WHITE/ OTHER

Fran Lock

Published 2022 by the87press

The 87 Press LTD

87 Stonecot Hill

Sutton

Surrey

SM3 9HJ

www.the87press.co.uk

ISBN: 978-1-7399547-8-9

Design: Stanislava Stoilova [www.sdesign.graphics]

For Marty

CONTENTS

HORSE FLESH

generational poverty:

alternate faces/ identical fates. alternate faces/ identical fates.
alternate faces/ identical fates. alternate faces/ identical fates.
alternate faces/ identical fates. alternate faces/ identical fates.
alternate faces/ identical fates. alternate faces/ identical fates.

+

i thought it would go on forever. and it did. it does. through
its traces, through its aftermath, its effects of repetition
and deferral. *trauma time* is recursive and hiccuping:
not a *continuum* but a *circuit*. it is never not happening
now. which is also the deviant time of the poor: we live a
concentric series of looping routines, through and across
time, that nevertheless are subject to every conceivable kind
of disruption, encroachment or glitch. poor time is eternally
delayed, suffused with a dolent expectancy: we wait, but we
wait for nothing. hours distend, weeks compress. we cannot
use our time. but our time is *used,* in a continuous cycle of
exhaustion and recovery. yet poor time is also immediate and
provisional: trained as we are to understand the world as not
for us, we have no real *future* into which we might project
ourselves. we live incrementally, from month to month,
from moment to moment. in part, this is the end result of a
long socio-economic precarity, but it is also an imaginative
failure: where exists the time or place not actively hostile
to our existence? we cannot enter the reflective time of the
middle-class, whose material security affords them the space
to be idle; who are *permitted* idleness by virtue of their status

as morally and spiritually superior beings. the time of the poor is wasted time, that is *waste* time, that is treyf time. the state is both entitled and obligated to use *up* our time: we do not *require* leisure because we are not capable of *spending* it *profitably*. we have no long-term desires, we cannot appreciate and so do not deserve travel, culture, art or nature. our pleasures are waste pleasures, treyf pleasures, compulsive and crude: the joyless gratifications of sex, food, and alcohol; the narcotised stupor of daytime television. we are taught to be ashamed of our idleness. we are told that to rest is *lazy*. we internalise this to a dangerous degree. we live under a system in which full employment is literally impossible, and yet the unemployed are daily, publicly shamed. productivity fuses to personhood along a ragged seam of skin, a mouth sewn shut. *i am a burden*, you said, *i'm fuck all use to anyone*. how to inhabit those hours emptied of labour, your hard earned skills left to rot in your hands? the days fill up with themselves, with a past you're condemned to repeat, with everything and everyone you have ever lost. *trauma time*, the traumas experienced *by* the poor. and the trauma of *being* poor: our prole *nachträglichkeit*.

+

i am asked if i'm writing a book. am i 'finally' working on my monograph? is it a 'book-book' or is it 'just poetry'? i am asked if i have ever considered fiction, autofiction, life-writing. so-and-so is doing a screen play. did i read such-and-such's collection of essays? blah-blah. *kif-kif*.

how to tell them, i am only writing a book where *book* is to *writing* what *scar* is to *wound*. where *book* demands the *scar* but refuses the *wound*. where the *scar* becomes a denial of the *wound* that produced it. how you learn to say: i remember that i was in pain, i do not remember *being* in pain. and *scar* is the glittering skin of affect. where the *scar* is empty, smooth and clean. refigured, devoid. where the *scar* is pure. how should i write, when the pen pushes back at the hand that holds it? it is not *the story* that refuses to be *told*. it is the *big idea* of the *book* that refuses *the story*; it is literature itself that resists and evicts me. put it another way: there is no *story*, there is only the *wound*. the *wound* cannot be said to *story*, speaking the *wound* picks open the scab.

what wound? i am asked. be more specific, more detailed, more 'particular', more 'precise'. what was it *like*? tell us *what happened*. little misery memoir. all the artifice that pretends to memory. traumatic memories are fragmented, i explain, difficult to describe. they are often inconsistent, inaccurate, lacking in contextual details; they – what trauma? i am interrupted. people can accept that poverty creates and exacerbates the conditions in which traumatic events occur, but they struggle to see poverty itself as traumatic. to see poverty as trauma. the *bad things* that happen to poor people are effects without cause. *ghost*, where the *ghost* is equally *haunted*. by the presence of the dead. by the presence and the possibility of death. the *spectre of poverty* that hovers over the living poor and is everywhere rejected. the living poor, rejected, themselves become *ghostly*, spectral, a fever dream. to persist inside of culture as a poltergeist or *boggart*; spoken around with superstitious fear, approached but never met. insubstantial. absent subjects. seen through, seldom seen. the rocking chair rocks by itself. this *wound*. and the *haunting* of diminishing returns whereby i haunt myself. to leave, to step through the magic mirror into *life*, *real life*, but to find no future there, to find only the same hole at the centre of all my escape fantasies. afraid of forgetting, exhausted by the impossibility of forgetting: doubled, split, hopelessly divided in my failed attempts to become someone else. i reach an irreconcilable impasse. i am stuck. if i push the past down inside of me, it surfaces time and again in symptomatic *ghostsings* of syntax, structure and sound. this is the *wound* that the *book* is trying to bury. i am not writing a *book*. i am opening the sutures it suits you to mistake for *scars*.

+

in my dream i have a hair. as i pull it out, i begin to unravel, starting from the mole at the corner of my mouth. i worry away at myself until i hold my face in my hands. my face is a mound of string: damp, steaming and hempy. more garden twine than *true* string. so as not to waste it, i carry my face into the garden and commence lashing cane poles to trellises. i will plant tomatoes. i will plant deep beds of *bearded lady* in honour of myself. i am very busy, and very content, and i work without self-consciousness. until somebody starts screaming. this is also about grief.

+

no, really. how grief is interrupted or prevented by a forced return of attention to the body. or, how i grew up to understand myself as some kind of magical animal, both sacred and taboo. to be always conscious of my unacceptable body: its excesses of odour, hair, and flesh. its dirt and its smell, its *feral* visibility. some words that constellate around me: ugly, slut, skank, slag, chav, dyke, pikey, cunt, munter, minger, whore, mick, bitch, scum, dog, fat, gypo, witch, cow, queer, rough, filthy, freak. in the vernacular of insult are class, race and sexuality unconsciously, insistently conflated. sometimes there are no words, and i am followed instead by a series of whoops and grunts, animal noises sharpened to suggest my physical resemblance to pigs or dogs or monkeys, and to mimic my accent, mocked as a sub-human babble. these petite little persecution plays were not for me. they were *at* me, i was their *object*, but not their intended audience. kids were doing their hate at me to assuage something between one another, to appease something within themselves. something they'd learnt, something they knew without knowing. to be *ugly* was not merely a *failure*, and thus an occasion for ridicule, but a *betrayal* to be rooted out and punished; a wilful rejection of *whiteness*. that is of the sleekness and symmetry from which an ideal *white* identity was constituted, and in which shape *white* aesthetic judgements were moulded and cast. i could not know this. i was still a child. i hadn't read bourdieu, who says that physical capital is the ability of dominant social groups to define their bodies and lifestyle as superior, worthy of reward; as symbolically and literally the embodiment of class.[i] who tells us that capital spawns capital; that through the insidious workings of privilege, physical capital is converted into economic capital. and round and round. i carried the marks of both my poverty and my *otherness* in my body. i carry them into adulthood. as a working-class woman, my lack of cultural, symbolic, economic or social capital compels me use what physical capital i have to exist in the world. thus my body traps me, as surely as the manual labourer is trapped, in a social world from which there is no escape. poor bodies wear down, wear out. class is a form of built-in obsolescence, which for women is also sexual, reproductive, and domestic. bodies without agency, autonomy or privacy. something stays. i avoid mirrors, cameras, crowds. cover my mouth when i laugh. i never eat in public or in front of strangers. i cannot look at myself naked. what bodies are: sites and sources of shame. innate shame, and the shame accreted around their use. something stays. it isn't the names used to and about me, it is their daily iteration, their multiplicity and profusion. my body does not belong to me. it is a form of public spectacle. it is flabby, pasty, coarse and stinking; seeping, stunted, crooked, gross. but it is – must be – endlessly available, whether the object of lust *or* revulsion. i am a hair-shirt made of myself. i feel their eyes on me, flesh-flies hatching maggots. all of the time. and grief, grief like sex is a *letting go*, requires a relaxation of this wary self-policing vigilance. but something stays, and mourning stalls as i am returned to my body. and the sight of myself, seen, with horror. to live as a punchline divorced from the joke. i shall make nothing grow. i shall make nothing grow.

+

look at me, sitting here like the booby prize in a meat raffle. say the words, and all the poison flows back into my mouth like fire into a foxhole.

+

i am writing a charm for a lasting enmity. these weapons of the weak. these powers you impute to me return three-fold and three by three. i have seen behind your poet's cesspit epigraph, found out beneath my own tongue, a cache of execration. *katadesmoi*, dear. imperishable curses. picking a private apocalypse into tin: this fate is a bicycle built for two. there's you, with the ground in your mouth, and cancer in your shanks. there's me, prone to wanton maledictive fits, set upon by crows. i follow you, through all your low-slung sunless days of harshed buzz and unconvincing laughter. i was hauled before the mirror, and the mirror is a magistrate, setting the bone of chill attention thus. and a white whey leaked between my teeth. tell me again about *god*, curing the sick with his lantern jaw. *corrective*. one day dear, *you* will be the body in the stocks, conspicuous with stones, your black eye the slow blink of an *irish kiss*. you don't know the half of it. mine are the old gods, old prayers, women crudely starred with sainthood: sara e kali, gran brigitte, carving their horny injunctions into mould. mine are the *old hands*, would strangle the piano into song. warm palm wine and ripened fruit. poitín, the sweat you lick from satan's lacquered tash. down midnight's disappointed drag, to glow with *leoht unfæger*, your heart alive with fratricidal raptures three am. at candy bar through feats of fickle fucking to become general under-secretary of the Society for Cutting Up Men. is the doggiest butch in this slum. dear one, they tried to razor the rad from my fem, these kids of fervent paradox, these better-clowns-than-you-have tried. i grew wings of rotary flame. let them come back later, let them try again. and look at *you*, in a lunar landscape of cheerless success, your skin the very refusal of fur. i become a hyena. a hyena is a sugared lunatic. the bloody stain offends the dress. she is the only wedding she is wearing, a garbage barge abandoned to its glamours, lit on fire like belfast. hyena is the raciest belle, has come to hate you, your pittances and small reprieves. to insist and to refuse. for the eye to swim in your empty head like a crouton in soup. these things i bring you. from the ulstery dust of my fathers fathers, mothers mothers. i hatchet my way to the centre of your fear, your immaculate lawns. i become an axe to your kitchen island. i never thought i'd have it in me, but discovered within myself a *late flowering*, packing my pockets like hard lemon candy. and a trench of grief, a trenchant grief. may the tumour that destroys you bear my likeness. may your back be the next border that i step.

+

the most common and immediate response to such poetry

7

is: *the fuck was that?* people understand rage. targeted rage. tied to an overt performance of identity. but this, i am told, is 'oblique', 'diffuse', 'directionless'. why are you so angry? what are you angry *about?* it isn't enough to say *everything*, every*one*. they do not wish to be included. say *straight men, straight white men, say cis, het,* say *the system,* say *tories, the poliss.* don't say the ambient conditions of neoliberal culture, don't say *the interactions that create the climate,* or *the climate that makes such interactions possible.* say *micro-aggressions.* don't say *the macro-aggression these micro-aggressions are evidence of.* how perfect strangers start conversations with me about the taste of horse flesh. for whom the horse is sacred. whose boys were centaurs, gleaming themselves through fire one time. *horse* is the opposite of *indifference,* a state of speaking grace made sinew. could no more eat a horse than ride a scorpion. perfect strangers ask me about dog fights, and ask me about "grabbing", and ask me about tyson fury. perfect strangers ask me about bloody sunday, and gerry adams, and the good friday agreement, and the murder of lyra mckee. perfect strangers ask me about "child snatching", and fortune telling, and house breaking, and childhood sexual abuse. i razor my way through the world with my teeth, apocryphal caliban. they say me to mistake, over again. they write me on walls, inside of a headline. all these repetitions multiplied into myth. they ask me about horse flesh. again.

Q: tell me about the taste of horse flesh.

A: it tastes like the cindermost ash of english. it tastes like spitting on a rush cross. it tastes like the telephone, emptying his death into me, an earache from the infrasound. it tastes like the pain and the possibility of working-class bodies. of irish bodies. it tastes of our squalid survivalist energy, a grubby bud of lace forced beneath the tongue. it tastes of *foreign bodies* and *inoperable bullets*, of inoperable bodies and foreign bullets. it tastes of carnival. it tastes of carrion. it tastes of the mouth filled up with the savour of its own decay. it tastes of stale wafers and warm wine. it tastes of the comely fascist who parts her poker face to tell me i have *reclaimed black thought for white discourse*. it tastes of *white/other*. when *other* cancels *white*. when *white* obscures *other*. it tastes of erasure: squared, halved. it is wearing this *white* and knowing the difference. it tastes like the briny suction of the sea. it tastes like the cringe of privilege and a caravan on fire. it tastes of gaffer tape and medical gauze. it tastes like the spaces between the words. i have this taste instead of language. my voice is the sound of my teeth tearing horsey flesh.

+

as you might say, *fragmentary*. when i read the word *fragmentary* i picture the dark asemic glyphs of cut hair curling onto kitchen lino. or i picture the hoover bag bursting, unburdening itself of archive. or i picture those frail scabs of gnostic parchment pinned under museum glass. where *fragments* are precious survivals of a devastated whole. where *fragments* are the flakes and discards of a body that rejects them. as you might say, *disjecta membra*. which is also *scattered limbs*, s*cattered members*, *remains*. as horace says: *the dismembered limbs of the poets*. the remnants and the residues of culture, and the traces of the people who produced it. when i read the word *fragmentary* i think about *four gre-e-en fields*, ploughed into boundary. and i think about bodies and the easy violence with which they are sundered. where *fragments* are also crumbs, *breadcrumbs*, clues. where poetry is forensis, tender and interminable. to scrape together, to break apart, to break away, to pierce, to part, to *break forth*. as if we might emerge into truth through ruin (we won't). read instead the redactions and the absences, the elisions and the lies as a kind of *negative evidence*, as myriad signs of erasure and eclipse. read against the cluttered tongue, crowded out of itself, the gaping space it halts at. true: trauma exhausts our rhetorical resources. false: that trauma silences those who experience it. no, but a surplus of speech, compulsive and repetitive. to be sullen and discursive in turns, to laugh, to cry, to scream and slur. leaden pedantry or manic gabble. verbigeration, perseveration, echolalia-alia-alia. and yet to come to the end of our invention without ever reaching or naming the *thing* we are trying to describe. it is not the case that trauma is or must remain *unspoken*, rather that any attempts at intelligent representation fail at, or are failed by, the limits of language. i arrive at the centre of the labyrinth, the stuttering, stammering core, and i come to a grinding halt. obsessive, ecstatic, i retrace my steps, i rewind and replay again and again each strategy of failed escape. i am pressed by the maze, pursued through the maze, and a minotaur is made of –

+

Q: and a minotaur is made of?

A: horse flesh.

+

i left london when i could no longer recognise the city. he left ireland when it refused to recognise him. i map our landscapes now by what is missing. by which i mean, i map our landscapes by what i miss, by whom. and how to say by the time he was old enough to meaningfully grieve his childhood, the sites and settlements of that shared experience no longer existed; his past was not meaningfully registered upon public space, was written over by an iconography of grieving from which he felt excluded. his experience of loss was unaccommodated by any of the available nationalistic, religious, or sectarian scripts. if grief and the act of remembrance are experienced in and through physical spaces both public and private, then what should that mean for those of us with a vexed relationship to such spaces? ireland devours her dead, folding them into her own mythology, inscribing their presence onto civic space. unless they are the *unacceptable* dead, the dead who do not fit the narrow arc of her nationally determined story. sing traveller dead, queer dead, junkie dead. within settled communities the legacy of sectarian violence is explicit and readily legible, scored upon public space through acts of myriad vandalism and memorialisation; the demolition of buildings, the securitisation of streets. for sedentary communities buildings capture the continuity of collective experience, they stage and re-emphasise a shared cultural heritage. in the north of ireland in particular, public artwork interacts with personal histories; mediates and facilitates the uncanny experience of memory between individuals and their wider communities, between these communities and the wider world. traveller, homeless, or vulnerably housed communities, whose settlements are, by their very nature, transitory, leave no corresponding trace or wound on the physical landscape. if public space is a container for cultural heritage, then those with no stake in that space, their histories, their memories, remain forever uninscribed. if the city is a body, how will we show where it hurts? to grieve is to grieve inwardly, invisibly. it is to find no place of recognition for your pain. and now gentrification, erasing both the past and the future for *all* poor and working-class communities. there are, as jahan ramazani notes, distinct *hierarchies of grievability*, kinds of grief, and grieved for subjects it is not acceptable to speak of or to mourn.[ii] gentrification is both a denial of persons and a refusal of their pain. we are blocked, at every step, on every level, from releasing this pain: how and where are we to mourn our lost, whose lives are characterised by the provisional, the precarious, the marginal and impermanent? how do we grieve poor, queer, vulnerably housed and homeless subjects? how do we reckon with the trauma of that grief, when trauma, by its very definition, renders problematic the possibility of representation? how is trauma to be told when, through contact with traumatic experience, individuals lose their ability to fully apprehend or integrate the memories of those experiences; when they are unable to give a coherent or consistent account of those experiences to others? how is grief to be rendered visible when the trauma of that grief is itself entangled in acts, official and unofficial, of forcible removal, denigration and erasure? ultimately, where do we even go to grieve once our landscapes are concreted over, our sites broken up, our communities dispersed, our squats torn down, our bars closed down, our dancehalls gentrified, our districts socially cleansed? we can exist nowhere, in our native place nor our chosen home. eisenstein writes that separation is built into the social and physical fabric of neoliberal society, and that those of us now living will never experience community because community is 'incompatible' with the highly specialised work, and estranged faceless dependence of modern capitalism. 'the groundwork of life' he says, is 'anonymity and convenience.'[iii] but *we* had community. before the pathological conformity of neoliberalism, *we* had each other. and we were not raised for convenience or anonymity; we don't know how to live in this world. from ireland to a council flat in london, forced out of the flat when his mother died; squatting in camden, moved on by security goons in black bomber jackets so that the area could be *renovated, renovated around*, subsisting, existing, becoming thinner and thinner, drinking to eclipse because to work these days you must be documented, accounted for, filed and stamped in fucking triplicate. in the end, only able to answer rejection with rejection, he ghosted and was gone. and i was left to this cartoon necropolis, doing me back to me as it shoved me out. evicting the poor from even poverty, the marginal from the margins.

+

how this too tastes of horse flesh.

+

and everything tastes of horse flesh.

+

my thesis: a charter of christ, written on horse flesh. in stinting rooms of stifled sap i dedicate my belligerent labour to a god-shaped stain on the ceiling. to teach is to grieve. at one remove. remote. erudite, distraught, in a faustian pact with some pale, defeatist textbook. *work makes enmeshment*, will organise these silences into consent. they barely know me. will service instead some pulsing bliss. odysseyed attention, wrested then anaesthetised. i am walking the white thread of a practiced vertigo. *are you listening to me?* man thumbs the eyes of his devices closed. GIFs of a gouching vigilance he sends to girls. sleaziest meme in a slaughter house. >> *self: how did you find that last exercise?* student #1: i found it rather contrived. *self: that's not a useful comment. obviously it's contrived, a workshop is not an organic and spontaneous response to the world. the academy is contrived, all our systems of organisation are contrived, the fact you're wearing an ugly polyester shirt is contrived, this moulded plastic chair is contrived, the signal nature of late stage capitalism is contrived. what does that mean?* << they want to be cupped and coaxed, want an amorous cache of girls, are horny, bored, furtive and compelled. are deft and splayed. are waiting to be escorted through the spinning doors in the opposite direction to their money. where wealth is a cartwheeling *fait accompli.* surfeit, duress. detained, curtailed, adjudicated, hacked. all of the above. the movement of one supremely itemized body through space and no-space. tracked. *self are you listening to me?* he mime's malfunction's shrug. >> student #2: you didn't explain that clearly. you're not being clear. where can i fill up my water bottle? why are there no refreshments provided? i didn't respond to the promp you gave, so i wrote this instead. you're bullying me. you're a bully. you're an elitist bully. you're a racist elitist bully. why are lesbians transphobic? you're transphobic. radscum, i'm not reading that. << with a *fuck you*! balloon in lieu of notes. i am trying to teach, but my mouth will not rake up the right sounds, the right names, and i'm up all night, paring a nerve like a nail, touching the world through gloves of numb affect. and fitful with defeat, speaking with the frigid exactness of a bad hangover in short bursts, finely calibrated. sometimes it is good, but i know i smell of horse flesh. i know that they know. my smile is a cloud of flies, i have eight white legs like a spider, i climb from my cradle of copper wire to squat on a desk called *teacher.* outside there is a protest. strenuous plainsong piped through fake white ipod buds. nine yellow hi-vis inscribed against empathy. where *all lives* and *no lives* and no one is listening. they run down the darkened jetties of themselves and jump. i cannot help them. i cannot help myself. and all this fairly stinks of horse flesh, horse fair, an unfair flesh. the horse *is the self-consumer* of its whinnying.

the horse devours itself.

+

as you might say *fragmentary*, if fragmentation is the result of trauma. if fragmentation is a defense *against* trauma. if fragmentation is the trippy nectar trauma makes in language. by which i mean, work without flow, the lumberjack song of whatever we create. by which i mean, shut up, who's telling this thing anyway.

i inhabit an enchantment; my day is filled with fairy tale endeavours: to empty the well with a broken sieve, to pass through a keyhole to the secret garden, to spin hemp into gold, to hold a needle of ice in my mouth so that it does not melt, to hold his death within the loving compass of a language that daily attempts to disown or evict me.

+

put it another way: there are three kinds of miracle: 1) *proeter naturam*, that is outside the ordinary course of nature, as when elias brought fire from heaven, as when the sick man is cured without medicine. 2) *contra naturam*, that is contrary to nature, without falling completely outside the realm of its wildest possibilities, as in the resurrection of the dead. 3) *supra naturam*, that is an occurrence so surprising as to require a complete suspension of the laws of nature; events that could never occur naturally, as in the sea parting or the sun standing still on command. replace the word 'miracle' with the word 'language'. replace the word 'language' with the word 'english'.

+

or, when i worked within the academy i would have endless meetings with people who persistently confused *language* and *english*. and stranger still, sometimes a man would use the phrase "pedagogic encounter" to describe teaching a class of first year bas. he would use this phrase without irony, when we were the only two people in the room. he would smile as he picked me up for my mispronunciation of *hegemony*, which i could not help but split into *hedge* and *money*, which made perfect sense to me. *hedge* being shelter and boundary; to defend and to surround, to limit and to qualify. *hedge* is to enclose and to separate, but its best self is the horny, regal green amen of spring. my doing the word wrong brings this last in with it. it shouldn't. my accent isn't strong, but it still, i am told, "mangles" some words hopelessly. *mangles* is a word appropriate to washer women.

+

how to say *i entered the academy* by stealth and by assault, by treachery and trespass, and no small measure of stubborn bloody-mindedness. to slither into their world through the eye of a needle, through the eye of a storm. on the afternoon of my initial interview i arrived early. as i waited outside i overheard – because i could not help but overhear – the conversation going on within. this was how i learnt that i would not secure funding, that my proposal was not "strong enough". this is how i learnt about the scepticism with which both my commitment and abilities were regarded. there is a mysterious alchemical process called *completion*, and i was *unlikely* to *complete*. to *complete* is to finish, but to *be* complete is also to be consummate and whole. from the latin to *fill up* or to *fulfil*. having *never* been filled or full or whole, i walked in fear of this failure. i sweat bullets. i give off the sour reek of weakness. my mouth goes dry. i had to sit that interview with clenched jaw, staring fixedly ahead. to blink would have been to cry. and to *cry* not in terms of tears, but in paroxysms of wounded animal ululation. i wanted this with such all-consuming intensity. i drifted somewhere above my body while a reedy séance-voice i did not recognise attempted to account for my work and to justify my presence, my existence, my right to take up space, this space, *any* space.

+

i did not know how to say these things. daily life had been composed of such accountings, but with fiendish variations: there is no all-purpose script. i'm talking about what poverty *requires* of us. i am talking about the exhausting demands and duties of "otherness". how we must develop an intimate acquaintance with the power of language. how we must live a continuous negotiation for resources or support, or to evade negative attention. being poor, and being other, people make assumptions about the kind of person you are, how you deserve to be treated, what you have and haven't a right to. these assumptions are embedded in – transmitted through – the words they use to and about you. they have material consequences, those words. we live at the mercy of that, between various kinds of coerced performance, learning to speak and to hear with infinite subtlety and precision in order to survive. but the ground is always shifting. our performances conflict, compete and undermine each other. they are meant to. our failure is part of the design. language plays tricks, lays traps. english does. *the* english. england. which forces us into a state of fevered *fragmentation*, then denounces our cunning, our hustle, our many "lies" and "cheats", our lovely sleights and feints.>> on the internet a latina woman's rage goes viral when she is told by her professor "this is not your word". it is one word, and that word is *hence*, and *hence* doesn't fit the vernacular performance of latina identity he feels entitled to from her. others need to learn to live on the receiving end of *hence*. as in *get thee.<<* i did not know how to say what i thought i deserved, or expected, or hoped for. i had no language in which to frame my desires. my future was a self-shaped hole i kept falling towards. *poor time* inoculates against ambition. i could only pretend to be them, to anticipate and mimic, however imperfectly, and thus erase myself, my reason, my meaning and my purpose. "otherness" is enacted in the very moment it is wiped out.

+

i could not say that i had come as a supplicant in response to an urgent need to locate or invent a form that would fold my graphorrea into his dyslexia to enact a tender politics of illegibility. *these* are not *my* words.

+

maybe it is not a fairy tale, but a transformation chase like in the lady and the blacksmith: where the "lady" is always the other, a fugitive through form, smaller and smaller until she cannot recognise herself, until her best defence against capture is to disappear altogether. you avoid becoming a victim by *volunteering* for annihilation. in the new discourse of post-everythingness we are meant to call this *agency*.

+

this is not what i meant to say at all. i have a conversation that goes like this: *i am trying to teach myself irish.* why? *because i feel its lack in me. because i am not sure english can be forced to hold these feelings.* but isn't irish a dead language? *no!* [with a certain obstinate pride] *it is threatened, but it is still spoken, it is still sung.* i meant that very few people speak it now. it can't adapt. it is a stale language. *is that a measure of how alive something is? how many people make use of it? is aliveness, then, an instrumental quality?* but who would you speak it with? *to myself, mostly.* and what would be the point of that? *for my mouth to be more than a basket of knives.*

when i talk *about* gaelic i ask myself: what is the difference between a dead language, and the language of the dead? i mean a language *for* the dead. i mean a language for a dead fell foul of english. i mean a language for marty. i mean, yes, irish, so we can talk to each other without the freight of pain carried inside of english, but more that we may address our dead on their own terms. no, so that they might speak to and through us. replace the word 'gaelic' with the word 'miracle'. by which i mean a language that brackets both the living *and* the dead in an enduring supernatural communion. by which i mean the *doing* of language as a temporal glitch and an act of solidarity that makes those other others present in the present. too often irish is presented as an exquisite corpse, its body marred by dirty revenant survivals. as if it were possible to separate that *völkisch* longing for a mythic hibernian past from what people make and are within the now: politics, pop-music, shite decisions. that is, irish as an impure and irresistible form of poetry that threads itself through english. in remix and mutation. what irish feeds and feeds from. shelta, in fact. my court of miracles.

+

i could not account for myself. that is, i am unacceptable *as* myself, and unconvincing as one of them. i bought my open door. in which *money* is inseparable from my bleachy hands and constant cold; from my five o'clock start and my vague smell of dog. in which *money* is inseparable from my unheated house, from the mildew and mould, from twelve hours a day in an airless room; from the boarded-up windows, the constant noise, from the concrete yard full of creepers and garbage. in which *money* means debt. in which *money* means *beg* or *borrow* or – i am a funnel for *money*. the *money* i funnel is filtered through the clammy gills of the academy. the academy becomes a keeve, sifting the wormy white pulp of my poverty for the golden curds of money. no, the academy becomes a centrifuge, separating out the ruby blood of *money* from the gross green bile of my poverty with a squeamish velocity. the academy refines and disguises my *money*. i would not recognise my *money* now if it slapped me in the face. i have failed to transform, but my *money* has transformed, and maybe after a certain time has elapsed, my *money* will transform me. the academy says you must *live what you love*: must shackle your identity to your work output so inescapably and so intimately that nobody has to acknowledge the conditions under which your labour is extracted. my *work* is supposed to flow from the swoon of sheer love. and the academy in its turn will love me back. *money* moves inside this system invisible, unacknowledged. i must avert my eyes. don't look at the *money*! maintain the illusion! the *money* buys the illusion that there is no *money*, that the academy is still an academy and not a *market*. what *money* offers is what we might call the *complete girlfriend experience*, blurring the boundaries between a financial transaction and a romantic relationship. i ruin everything: draggle, bankrupt and proley, wearing my many shit jobs as a layered odour in my clothes, and banging on about *money* like i didn't get the memo. the poor make *money* visible, we expose the economic underpinnings of the system in which we operate. we puncture the illusion that art and culture are magically exempt from *money*, that the position and status of elites are the result of exceptional merit. they fucking hate that.

+

or should i being with how representations and discourses of "otherness" contain many contradictions? how the other is aligned to the abject, to squalor and dependency, criminality and need. yet the other is also exotic, it carries the scent of superstition, the undersong of savagery. there is a r/Romance to the other; there is a danger too. the other is destitute and wan, the uniform and institutional grey of generational poverty; the other is a swaggering clash of texture and colour, the super-saturated palette of extreme "bad taste". what creates "otherness" is not difference, but indeterminacy. the other *is* excess and exceeds itself. the other is without definition; the other multiplies definitions. what you might call *fear of the other* is only in part the fear of *specific* others. what you might call *fear of the other* is in fact the amorphous fear of "other*ness*", is fear *of* the amorphous, of the vague and unspecified. the menace and seduction of the other is that the other is *whatever you want it to be, baby, yeah*, is constituted afresh from desire or dread to suit your purpose. what i mean is: there are no others, there is only "otherness".

+

i am watching the roman polanski film *rosemary's baby*. it's a horror film, based on the ira levin book of the same name, in which mia farrow plays rosemary, a sweet suburban housewife, who is manipulated by her elderly satanist neighbours – with the complicity of her louse actor husband – into giving birth to the antichrist. i like the film, but it's a poem of irrational middle-class anxiety. in an early scene, guy and rosemary, this nice, young, upwardly-mobile couple, make fun of their neighbours, minnie and roman, for their mismatched dinner service, uncouth décor, and general lack of social awareness. there's a "book on a hook!" screams rosemary, "right next to the john!" as if this were the most uproariously funny thing in the world. later, she points out roman's pierced ears in a tone that embraces both scandalised amusement and a creeping suspicion of something sinister. minnie and roman are vulgar. *especially* minnie. she is loud, obtruding, importunate. and my god, she is nosey! she snoops and pries and pokes. she brow-beats and badgers and will not take no for an answer. she *literally* elbows her way into rosemary's apartment, asking the price of this or that without embarrassment or pause. her make-up is lurid, profoundly unsubtle; she is dressed without fail to an eye-popping extremity of gaudiness. her new york accent is penetrating, pungent of place, in stark contrast to rosemary's soft and modulated tones. before we see her we hear her: a hectoring voice through the wall, encroaching and interrupting even when not *physically* present, spilling out, spilling over, refusing to be contained. i fucking love minnie castevet. she is fear of the other made manifest. when rosemary and guy are sat there laughing at her, i think: *good, serves you right!* because i know what's coming and because i understand myself as minnie too. minnie is *common.* she is one of us, yet she will not, as you might say, *stay in her lane.* she grabs at power with both hands, dares to take by force what wasn't handed to her at birth. which is what her satanism is a cipher for.

+

fear minnie. fear and hate her. hate her like you hate the mcmansions of the newly rich. hate her like you hate the crass aesthetics of the working-class, of traveller girls, of drag queens, of any other others, because they amplify and satirise your own values; because they make explicit the morbid decadence of neoliberal culture, because they revel in and invert that decadence, because they *eat the rich*, because they cannibalise and parody "taste". or because they reject and deny the relentlessly naturalised "taste" of the white middle class. hate minnie like you hate the basely functional language of the poor, the frivolously-without-function language of the poor, the no-win never language of the poor. hate minnie like you hate the exuberant swagger of *yoot'* culture: style as a singular libidinal fury, erected against destruction. hate minnie like you hate the gutter punctuation of the tabloids, the florid sensational prose of *cheap fiction*. hate our strange rhapsodic surges, our chants, or moans and shouts. hate the argot of the other, which, like "otherness" itself embodies both degradation and extravagance. because this is *your* language, and we have sullied it with our coarseness and our crudities, from the *ghettos of low culture, from the scurf of the body corporate*. fear that english might gestate within your own mouth, changed: the monstrous child of an unnatural union. fear miscegenation with the dread of death. fear what is spread on breath, a pestilence, those words that rot the tongue that shapes them. fear what might be smuggled *inside* of language, the otherness inside of *you*. fear minnie, for minnie is the other who refuses to stay put in the otherness ascribed to her, who cheats and tricks her way out of subaltern otherness in good silver, a sought after apartment, furs and jewels. for minnie is brazen, and is shoving her social ascension in your face, rubbing your nose in the otherness you made her wear.

+

mary russo writes in *the female grotesque* that images of the grotesque body are exactly those abjected from bodily canons of classical aesthetics: 'the classical body is transcendental and monumental, closed, static, self-contained, symmetrical and sleek; it is identified with *high* or official culture [...] with the rationalism, individualism, and the normalizing aspirations of the bourgeoisie. the grotesque body is open, protruding, irregular, secreting, and changing.'[iv] the grotesque is an open *wound*, a denial of catharsis, a refusal of the pure. and who would choose to live inside this body? to wallow in the adulterated and uncanny identity of otherness? who could resist the pull of that self-transcending narrative, that aspirational rise to glory in which is shed all aspects of her former self?

+

as cynthia cruz has noted in *the melancholia of class* the grotesque bodies of the poor haunt middle-class imagination: sloppy and straggling, ill-disciplined and unrefined. the bodies of the poor are vague and amorphous too. a mob, a hoard, a *swarm* in which no one face is distinct or memorable.[v] and yet, the poor are improbably "ugly". by which is meant *marked by the world*, bearing the traces of labour, diet, environment, of hard life and ill use. the bodies of the poor are awkward and ungovernable, whether rough and roistering or weak and sickly. ciphers for criminality. or disease. or sin. infection vectors. typhoid maries. the sour whiff of moral contagion. for the other-other doubly so. how middle-class fantasies separate out the poor from their poverty so that being poor becomes a cause in itself. and blame becomes possible, and hate becomes possible. i read that british law was set up specifically to protect the property and persons of the elite from the *mobile vulgaris*. i read that the man who invented the idea of group madness, gustave le bon, cheered the destruction of the paris commune; dedicated his poisonous 1895 polemic *the crowd: a study of the popular mind* to "proving" that mass revolutionary movements were nothing more than a manifestation of collective insanity.[vi] mussolini was a big fan. goebbels was a big fan. i read thomas carlyle's gospel of work. i read herbert spencer say of the poor that 'under the natural order of things society is constantly excreting its unhealthy, imbecile, slow, vacillating, faithless members'[vii], that we are to be starved out like fever, exterminated like disease. george borrow referred to travellers as the scurf of the body corporate. here is evoked the diseased bodies of the poor white other. here is the other at metonym for a besieged and infected white*ness*. *scurf* is from the old english for *to gnaw*: to burrow under, undermine, to wear away with the termite teeth of poverty. *scurf* is also to *cut* and to *fragment*. the pure body broken up from within. the social body. and the body of language.

THEY SAID

'These people ["Abraham men" or "Pikers"] have frequently been confounded with the Gypsies, but are in reality a distinct race, though they resemble the latter in some points. They roam about like the Gypsies, and, like them, have a kind of secret language. But the Gypsies are a people of Oriental origin, whilst the Abrahamites are the scurf of the English body corporate. The language of the Gypsies is a real language, more like the Sanscrit than any other language in the world; whereas the speech of the Abrahamites is a horrid jargon, composed for the most part of low English words used in an allegorical sense' – George Borrow, *Romano Lavo-Lil* (1874).

+

'One can rarely be sure whether the word ["Gypsy"] is being used in its proper sense, to describe the obstinately surviving race of pure-bred Romanies – that is pure bred as one finds them in these times – who still uphold as best they can the nomadic traditions of their ancestors; or whether the true Gypsies are being lumped together with other social groups like mumpers, squatters and tramps.' – A. Fraser, 'The Gypsy Problem' from *The Journal of the Gypsy Lore Society, Third Series* (1953).

+

"it's not Irish, it's not English, it's just, well… it's just pikey" – From the film *Snatch*, by Guy Ritchie (2000).

"POGGADO JIB"[1] / DEAR GEORGE

dear george, just to say: i mistook my tongue. for a locust dipped in honey, for the cloudy surmise of a mushroom sublimed in its spores, for the scurvy vagabondage of a london night, for the airless distillery slang of ghosts. or for mícheál's hand as it slicked from me, for the wasting regime of hospitals, for us raw-boned boys, chewing the cud of conviction, those golden paddock-chancers, a chaser of dirt to go with the comment they swallowed. all of my life, i mistook myself for the wind in the weeds. with a stupid look, like a horse led lame to water. dear george, just to say: i saw myself this morning as a line of ants, as a string of beads. my sickle stunts, the cloudy part of pain, the way the starlings break apart like leaves of tea. this way we once had language: the horses' backs like pale anvils, a coke can dipped in the holy well, and kestrels, those aerial sadists always. george, we are not animals, and are animals, and saw ourselves in the decorous twilight of beasts. the wrens, the dogs, the foxes. the jinxes and the flukes. i travelled in torchlight the length of myself. i looked on us boys in gilded, gelded sullenness, how their lips cracked in want of a cross to kiss, loiterers in stale glory. dear george, to be a reaper of repeat offences, to be *spooky*, trailing a vaudeville doom for kicks. i was the swan's mother. i was the *tar baby's* midwife. writhing on a bed of wanton lilies, wrapped in plastic. do you not know me? having entered my tent, having asked me my name,

---

[1]After Victorian novelist and ethnographer, George Borrow, and other self-proclaimed "Romany Rye": who set themselves up as experts in and arbiters of "Gypsy" language and culture, coiners of the phrase "poggado jib" (or "chib"), which they translate as "broken tongue", to describe the degenerate speech of impure itinerants as opposed to that of the "true" or "pure" Romanies. Fuck those guys.

having issued your rokkering warrant. am i not stained by your bootsteps? here, where you trampled your epitaph into my skin, scholar of our pyrrhic kennings, mottos scrawled on the blade of an axe. said me to debris, convened your committee of sour regrets in my empty mouth. dear george, do you know me now? with *your* tongue dressed in all the finery of refusal, and many more here after, the arts council funding a thoroughbred *no!* and hoarse with warning. mícheál passing pinkly through an ugly medical threshold. where temperant assessors say *speak not your lumpen fury. speak not your cock-robin hiccup of song, traipsing through an aisling.* you've hung a sign from our language that reads *no irish need apply.* struck a match against exhaustion and burnt our papers by candlelight. same old. and the cherished repetition of a hand through a flame, through a plate-glass window, through a hole in our culture. how you sealed me tight against reply within the infamous skin of obituary, muttered my melt-weight to fraud, made me a bantering shadow: *counterfeit*, a bleak fate i cannot counter. to sew my fist in the deep pocket of my poacher's coat, i grow myself more blades than coins, more coins that fingers. do you know my name? broken, between pannier-paths and weirs, an axe, the hot dread of *halting*. i mistook my name for a spasm of magpies, for mícheál's hair, threshed by the weather, for pungent honey, for my mirage of fragile appetite. in a place of inhospitable reprieve, a pause, the lay-by where i gave my name, and dressed myself in a saint's shed skin. dear george, how it feels to be *scurf*, how language sweats out my infection my affect my affection syllable by syllable. i mistook myself for a woman, and the molten frontier of his stare for love. we took the cobalt altar of the night for ours. how the hedge hung sweetly on our nakedness. i mistook the road for my own, the long day swollen with oaths, the breath made feathery with effort, george, was this *never* ours? barefoot *in the wakehouse of the gaelic language*, as we said ourselves to error again and again, encore towards the dying fire. to be so repulsively dispossessed, like a naked snail, our songs have second-guessed the gutter. dear george, you may keep your purity. this is language made erratically with hammer blows. i met the morning in his mouth these tongues were never broken, george. our native grief, the cleave.

there is silence in the workshop, when the young woman asks me if i'm *sure* i'm white. silence, not embarrassed, but expectant. i do not know what to say. the question is too preposterous to parse: of course i'm sure, and of course i'm white. i am obviously white. i am flamboyantly white, *egregiously* white. on a purely physical level, i am sterile milk and silent film, a kabuki mask, a photocopied ghost, the palest thing in the fucking room.

+

that isn't what she meant. or, it is and it isn't. how to say? there's the white you are and the white you become. that is, the way my skin is supposed to be a shorthand, a shortcut, my passport to a shared language of whiteness, where the signifier "white" and the white identity it generates is affirmed and prescribed, where belonging is made and renewed, over and over, through various kinds of "white" performance. i had failed in my performance. if only for a moment, i had missed my cue. i did not correctly speak my symbols. i did not correctly speak my skin. i did not confirm the colour that is written on my face. why? something i'd said? the sounds i produced when i said it? or it was something *in* the poem: the shrine, the well, the names of saints, the wrenboys or the clootie tree, the raisins for the dead, how a heron is an omen bird? no. not exactly, not the *things* themselves, but my lack of ironic distance *from* them. i would be allowed as many ghosts and miracles as i could carry, as much god or nature as i could usefully stand, so long as they were being carted around inside the poem as dead lyric freight, as tools, as resources. "white" literary policy is the indiscriminate ransack of cultures, traditions and histories towards the enrichment of "white" art. theft without tenderness. what *i* had done wrong is seem to invest, believe, embody. i had just announced the earth was flat. i was screaming that the sky was falling down because an acorn had dropped on my head. i had breached the immaculate etiquette of scepticism, a certain connoisseurship. i appeared before them as credulous and unsophisticated: a superstitious peasant. the customs and beliefs of the "white other" are particularly irksome to these people because they disrupt the categories – "liberal", "progressive", "rational" – from which white middle-class identity is constituted. she glares at me, this woman. in that hot, bright room, under the spotlight of critical scrutiny, the unspoken assumptions that constitute my privilege are being stripped away. i spoke about my privilege in passing, and that's what prompted the question. yes, but am i *sure* i'm white? whiteness rules by effortful consensus. that is whiteness rules by coercive control; like any grand illusion, like any believable lie, it requires mass participation and continuous maintenance in order to function. the voice bodied forth in the poem was doing white wrong. "whiteness" itself cannot possibly be at fault. "whiteness" is above suspicion and beyond reproach. so am *i* sure?

+

or no, not exactly. it isn't the "magic". magic is allowed. you can be "witchy". within the contemporary lyric, the witch is rampant, but she's a cardboard cut-out, a papier-mâché mask, a line of affect. the white lyric witch is all surface: a trope, or a pose. she is not unrelated to her commercial sister, the consumer witch, whose magic – as douglas ezzy writes – is a kind of relentlessly optimistic self-help.[viii] this witchcraft empowers the individual, her poetry exceptionalises the figure of the witch as uniquely subversive and brave. when she suffers, her suffering is dignified and vivid. she's a hero, an ideal. her witchcraft is the work of an exemplary whiteness. persecuted, yes, but never broken, or abject. her witchcraft is effective and spectacular; she is without class and without context.

+

in *caliban and the witch*, silvia federici writes about the belief in magic in early european societies as a massive stumbling block to the rationalisation of the work process.[ix] magic functioned as a refusal of work, a form of insubordination and grass-roots resistance. women's claim to magical power in particular undermined state authority because it gave the poor and powerless hope that they could manipulate and control the natural environment, and by extension subvert the social order. magic must, therefore, be ground out of existence for the projects of church and state to be realised; poor and indigent women must be trampled underfoot. we talk about the witch trials as a form of femicide, but they were also a profound mechanism of social cleansing. witch-work is not the consolidation of individual power: it is class-resistance. it is what geraldine monk calls 'language magic', and its failure is the limits of that language, is the classed voice – its accents and grammar – raised in futile defiance against a monolithic legal eloquence, against the hegemonic english of church and state and law.[x]

+

so no, within the poem, the problem isn't the "magic". it's the ugliness of that magic, the brokenness of that magic; it is magic classed and concentrate in a body *without* power and *without* beauty, in a voice raised against the sanctioned syntaxes of good middle-class prosody. it is a meant and useless magic. and somebody calls the poem "intense". and somebody calls the poem "feral". what is meant by "feral"? i have an idea, for feral has followed me all of life. how old was i when i first heard "feral", as applied to children like myself? twelve or thirteen? and the signs in shop windows or the doorways of pubs: "no dogs! no gypos!" anywhere an equivalence is being drawn between certain *kinds* of people and certain *kinds* of animal. the idea of the dog, evoked in its most negative aspect, and the human other assumed to share those characteristics, to be dog-*like*: dirty and ungovernable, all fleas and teeth and unspecified menace. i have been "dog", and "mongrel", and "bitch" besides. the person subject to such metaphors is not merely being likened to the animal in question. rather the disgust felt towards the animal is being transferred to that person. we eat the sins of the rabid, the vicious, the promiscuous and mangy.

+

joan dunayer, writing in *animal equality: language and liberation*, talks about the process of dehumanisation, and the inherent speciesism necessary for this process to work: to reduce the human to the level of an animal, we must first account the animal as nothing. the brutalising treatment of animals is not merely cruel, but a necessary precursor to patriarchy, racism, homophobia, fascism, to all manner of violence and persecution.[xi] as a culture, we become accustomed to brutal acts by perpetrating them first against animals. we deaden the nerve with indifference and sentimentality both. and speciesism creates the *language* in which it is possible to dehumanise the other amongst us. you'll tell me the english are a nation of "animal lovers". no. the english love their pets. where "pet" is a kind of sentimental prosthesis, the opposite of "animal". all those nice, polite women in quilted gilets airbrushing their dog's genitals out of photos.

+

dunayer states that: 'the way we speak about other animals is inseparable from the way we treat them'.[xii] i'd go one further to suggest that the way we speak about other animals is often a *microcosm* for the way we treat them: within language and literature they become a semantic and rhetorical resource just as they are a resource within the world, where they are valued only as bodies, for the labour that can be extracted from them, for their reproductive capacities or for their flesh.

+

a fundamental cornerstone of western thought is the persistent imaginative yoking of animality and womanhood; transmitted through art and culture via the ideologically charged woman-as-animal metaphor: – cow, bitch, pig, chick, bunny, shrew, etc. – as josephine donovan notes in *the aesthetics of care: on the literary treatment of animals*, under patriarchy the feminised animal is 'an abject creature, upon whom are ascribed aspects of otherness.[xiii] we are already considered inferior for being women, but the female other is figured as doubly so for not living up to the woman she is supposed to be. the signifiers of race and class – everything from accent and grammar, to clothes, weight, the condition of our skin and teeth – are intimately linked to perceptions of femininity, sexual availability and moral worth. as a working-class, queer, and culturally marginal woman, i am evicted from the hallowed precincts of the feminine. which is also to say "white". my de facto status is non-woman, non-human, emphatically animal. "humanity" is a vexed category anyway. it has *always* excluded certain subjects from personhood: including women, the colonised, the marginalised, the maimed, any category of life that threatens the seamless structural integrity of society or language.

+

broken tongue / broken english. broken by what? by whom? by grief? by trauma? which – in the words of walter benjamin – is any rupture 'to the homogenous structure of experience'.[xiv] which is, then, an irreducible feature of "otherness", of being "othered". i think of lament, of the *caoineadh* or *caoin*: that extemporised oral practise, born out of moment; a porous form that suffers and seeps beyond the perceived enclosure of the printed page, beyond language, beyond the body. its sonic substance is the cry, the gasp, the compulsive iteration and the shocked silence. it is rage and longing. *elegy* is eloquent, articulate, it interprets and it orients. it also mediates. it translates grief for the individual, and it translates between that individual and their community in times of emotional stress. the elegy is a medium through which the work of mourning flows, and mourning is an act of assimilation: catharsis, from the greek verb to *purify*. to tidy up and socially situate our pain. "otherness" has no elegy. cannot be tidied. society wants neither our grief, nor our grieved-for subjects. we inhabit the howling phantom zone of inconsolable loss. to us the raw, recalcitrant and untranslatable traumas: the grief we bear as others and the grief of other*ness.*

+

to be lost. to be *lost for words.* to be *at a loss*, which implies an arrival, a mark on a map. stranded here, estranged inside of elegy too, inside of lyric. lyric, which inscribes order, which emphasises a highly selective and controlled mastery over its materials – linguistic and emotional. lyric derives its special status from this mastery; it produces controlled and tempered trajectories. stunning *arcs* of emotion, true, but definite arcs nonetheless. what to do who are unequal to this alchemy? i read that canonical elegy mirrors what are said to be the three stages of loss: first, there is a lament, where the speaker expresses grief and sorrow, then praise and admiration of the idealized dead, and finally consolation and solace. there is a neat and pleasing symmetry, the text reflecting human grief. only the text isn't a mirror. or if it is, it's a warped and distorted mirror. the way in which we use language is entangled in thought; it determines and it constitutes our intellectual operations; it can straight-jacket us, bind us to a normative performance of grieving we may feel excluded from, unable to live up to. there's a coercive insistence on healing, there is an instrumental eloquence. we cannot embody these values, these forms. how will we speak? how will we poem?

+

in ireland, between the seventeenth and twentieth centuries, the *caoin* was actively condemned by the church, and legislation enacted to prohibit its practice as a heathen "abuse". the *caoin* is a shape-shifter: identified within popular consciousness as a species of "feral" and pagan noise-making, a misrepresentation fostered by religious and occupying authorities in ireland, who frequently demonised its practitioners as animalistic, immoral, or crazed. but the *caoin* is also its own highly specific verse tradition, with its own rich set of tropes, its own particular aesthetic disposition. the roots of the word encompass the idea of beautiful musical singing and of disarticulate weeping.

the form compresses and enfolds both of these identities; speaking to the traditional practice of the *caoin*, and to its persuasive cultural myths. historically, criticisms of the *caoin* performed a nasty little janus-faced manoeuvre in which it was simultaneously despised for being heathen and wild, and disdained as "immoral", because it ritualized – and sometimes monetized – the process of grieving. the *caoin* was too unrestrained and artless to be quite proper, while at the same time too formalized to be authentic or sincere. because the caoin is embodied to a high degree, condemnation of the form also attached to its practitioners. it wasn't simply that the tradition was in some way disorderly or "bad", but that these qualities were the signal moral attributes of the women who performed it. *bean sídhe*. banshee. scald-crow. otherworldly woman issuing her *gol*, her omni-directional animal scream.

+

when i spoke my poem, my poem too was a *caoin*. an *i* leaked out of that poem: vulgar, backward and aberrant. i entered my telling as an animal. i enter the animal. the animal enters me, escapes me. i escape through a fur-covered arch in the animal. to reside within the animal. to write the animal. to *do* the animal in different voices, to pass *through* the animal to the other side of the animal. did i say *the animal*? i meant *the world*. to inhabit and assume the animal, to be overcome by the animal, consumed by the animal, the animal exposed.

+

"feral" follows into poetry too. it follows "edgy", "raw", and "fauve", thinly disguised as a compliment. it is a useful word: it allows middle-class critics to admit, without ever having to credit, the deep, strange basis of our creative practice, the practice of the other. "feral" persistently figures features as bugs, and disciplined choices as accidents of untutored energy. in this way "feral" preserves and naturalises the myth that rigour and innovation are solely the fruits of white middle-class literary production.

+

are you *sure* you're white? and i want to say: as opposed to what? by which you mean what? law-abiding? educated? cultured? correct? moral? what accretes around whiteness or abides within it? by "white" do you really mean "human" after all? do you mean more or less than skin? a shared fund of formal tics? those elegant lilting iambics? what belongs to me. that to which i belong. can carry, can claim. my text is insurrection, then? or not my text, but the sound of my text in my mouth, as inseparable from myself? they turn on me. in a polite and passive-aggressive sort of way. if *they* weren't so educated, if *they* weren't so cultured, if *they* weren't so moral, what then? the elite space can't scream "white n****r!" and they never would, would *they*? the work of their whiteness is covert, unconscious even, semi-conscious; invisible, refined and sly. but *they* do say "chav", don't *they*? not to my face, not usually, but they say it. and they do say "pikey". not british *or* irish, but both and neither. to look at i am *so* white that i disappear daily within the dense crush of *their* anglophile assumptions. yet i live within those categories as an alien other: strange, estranged inside of whiteness, because *they* don't mean me when they say "white". for them, "pikey" is a way of removing me from that select community of whiteness, a form of *lexical* cleansing. "pikey" is also an eviction, a banishment, a *get thee hence*, a spell of protection.

+

so how should i answer? to insist i share their skin is to support the value system that produced the question. but what else should i call myself? do i not benefit from being white? is *my* whiteness not my subterfuge? my protection? my disguise? i have brown and black friends who joke that i'm their "sleeper", that i'm doing deep-cover; i'm their penetration agent inside of academia, in literary space. they expose themselves to me, because i "pass" as one of them. but i'm not doing deep cover. i'm a coward, and there are times i've used my whiteness like a shield. subjectively, "pretending to be one of them" feels edgy and subversive. it isn't. it's a disavowal of the explicitly other. i can "pick my battles". i can opt-out, until i'm found out, until i open my mouth, say the wrong thing in the wrong way, until i give myself away. and i do, again and again. this isn't winning. this isn't "turning the tables". this isn't power. this is a naughty child resorting to cheap tricks because she cannot overthrow the adult order. her tricks benefit only herself, and not even herself in the long run. my human disguise is an empty room, a depthless stain. it consists of skin and sound, of everything i borrow back from *whiteness*.

+

in the workshop they are staring. and i want to say: that depends on what you mean by "white". and i want to say *anything* else less feeble than that. no. in truth, i want to howl like the animal i am. i want to punch her. i want to the smash furniture. i want to rip her to shreds with my teeth. my grandfather would say it's the same old shit since cromwell. in terms of mechanism, if not intensity. cromwell saw us as 'beasts'. john taylor metaphorized the killing of protestants by howling 'irish wolves'. heylyn wrote that the irish behaved 'scarcely like men'.[xv] and if a *taig* is an animal, a devil, or a demon, a *tinker* is a what? it *is* the same. how one time at school, a girl called me "terrorist". i found a dead crow and stuffed it into her bag during pt. maggots and blood got on all of her books. she screamed and i was delighted. one time a group of boys cornered me. they spat in a coke can and made me drink it. smeared dog shit on my chair. followed me home singing gypsies tramps and thieves. day after day. year after year. until i'd snap, because who wouldn't? but that's what they want: confirmation of your feral status, your dirty animality, your violence. your rage at their treatment of you becomes the very argument *for* that treatment. you cannot win. i never did. they stalk the empty space where sleep should be.

+

"feral" does the dirty work: was the occupying english argument for colonisation, displacement, transportation and murder. it was the school bully's rationale for pelting me with rocks. it was the teacher's excuse for sticking his hand up my skirt. it's boucicault and borrow, it's a million shitty "satirical" cartoons, where the irish are apes, alkies and psychos. simian biddies and fenian schemers; machete men, bomb-plotters, zombies and monsters. wolves. werewolves. are you *sure* you're white? in irish identity are class and ethnic hatred muddied and met. to live with this is to be pushed to the point of murderous fury, aware all the while that they want your anger, they want it because it confirms them in their low opinion of you. they want it so they can use it to justify your continued subjugation, your need to be "civilised", "occupied", "taken in hand". you are *men that god made mad, mad in limb and tongue.* their abuse of you isn't abuse at all. why, it's a public fucking service. and what has ireland done with this, but rolled its shit downhill? travellers are the irish it is permissible for even the other irish to hate. the animal's animal.

+

cromwell placed a bounty on the wolves in ireland. the last wolf was slaughtered there in 1786. when i talk about this everyone understands it as emblematic – that is, "poetic" – and sad. i *write* a poem in which i link the extinction of the wolf in ireland to the extermination of the irish language. i have my students write poems that link territory and tongue. i tell them that during *an drochshaol* the places where spoken irish thrived were hardest hit. i send them audio clips from the *endangered poetry project*, i get them to make lists of dialect words or local phrases linked to threatened nature or to disappearing trades, communities or customs. we talk about famine, slavery, climate violence. when i speak about the irish people or the romanichals sold as slaves to plantations in the americas by cromwell the reaction is confused. somebody asks me: did that *really* happen? where's your *evidence* for that?[xvi] the pain of white others has so often been weaponised as a defensive retreat from active solidarity, and i don't know how to say to my students: *that isn't what i meant* because the accusation is unconscious, the suspicion unexpressed.

+

travellerness exists in strange relation to irishness. and irish travellers exist in strange relation to other ethnic nomads. and when i say strange: "they're not *real* gypsies", someone says, "they don't even go anywhere." never mind that by-laws have made it equally illegal to settle or to shift; that the halting sites provided by local councils are inadequate by any practical or sanitary measure. and never mind that there are no "*real* gypsies", that "gypsies" is from the presumed imposture of romani people, masquerading as egyptians, "counterfeit egyptians", christians on a long pilgrimage of penance. "gypsiness" is linked to deception and pretence in a variety of ways within english imagination: the lies that romani people tell, and the greater deceit of pretending to be "gypsy" as practised by "vagabonds" and "indigent irish". irish travellers entered british legislation in this way.[xvii]

+

every time priti patel opens her mouth a little more shit seeps into the world, a little more sunlight is leached out of it: the home office consultation on criminalising trespass and increasing police powers against unauthorised encampments came hard on the heels of a report exposing the enormous unmet need for pitches on public traveller sites in england. according to the report, released by the leading national charity: friends, families and travellers, over 1696 households were on waiting lists for pitches on public sites. there were a meagre 59 permanent pitches and 42 transit pitches or halting sites available nationwide.[xviii] the new laws would mean that families living on unauthorised encampments could face fines, prison sentences, and removal from their homes, simply for having nowhere else to go. the number of caravans deemed to constitute an unauthorised encampment has been reduced in number from six to two. two. police will direct these caravans from any site on which they have no permission to stay, even when there are no alternative stopping places. the right of british ethnic nomads to live in a caravan home is recognised by the european court of human rights and protected in the uk courts under the human rights act 1998. yet the tories did not – do not – care. patel does not care. her now infamous comments during an online meeting with jewish leaders in september 2020, branding traveller families as inherently "criminal and violent", are now well documented. during the tory clampdown in the early 1990s two thirds of traditional, informal halting sites for travellers were sealed off. in 1994 the criminal justice act repealed the duty of local authorities to provide official sites for travellers. an obvious solution to unauthorised encampments would be to return this statutory duty to provide sites. if nothing else it would seem to be the cheaper solution, demanding less enforcement and provoking fewer legal challenges. it would make damage to public land less likely too: much of this happens due to deliberate obstacles being placed in the way of access points, and to a lack of public amenities at these unauthorised sites. most importantly it would allow travellers and their families to access vital public services. but patel doesn't care about that. as the threat of eviction undermined the ability of traveller communities to comply with coronavirus regulations, many were asking themselves how long before the pandemic was utilised as an irresistible argument for forced assimilation, and the dispersal of communities? existing sites, whether privately run or managed by local authorities, are often located close to motorways, major roads, refuse tips, industrial estates or sewage works: undesirable locations all, and damaging in unique ways to the health of the travellers who live there. ethnic nomads in britain die on average between seven and twenty years earlier than the rest of the population, and their health outcomes are significantly worse. a 2016 report sponsored by the national inclusion health board noted that 66% of roma travellers had bad, very bad, or poor health; poor air quality, proximity to industrial sites, asthma and repeated chest infections in children and older people were noted in nearly half of all interviews. health access has always been complicated and fraught for people living in traveller communities. this has led to a lack of early diagnosis, resulting in poorly managed chronic conditions. people are going to die. we've got all the statistics and all of the arguments, but people are going to die. other others are going to die. this is not my pain. that is, this is the context for my pain, not the pain itself. it isn't daily for me. i don't live this. but i live *with* this, in sensitised and troubled association with this. and people keep asking me how i feel about this. and i give them my facts and my arguments and my statistics and people say: no, but how do you *feel*?

+

halting site/ halting state/ halting site/ halting state/ halting site/ halting state/ halting site/ halting state/ halting site/ halting state/ halting site/ halting state/ halting site/ halting state/ halting site/ halting state/ hating site/ halting state/ halting site/ halting state//

+

there's a poem, a hateful little thing of victorian vintage, about how it's not the "honest gypsy" who is to blame for your crops failing, or your livestock going missing, or your house being robbed, or whatever. it's the "irish tinker" that did it. mudblood. mongrel. is there anything worse you could be? well, maybe one thing. a recent hashtag: #poshratandproud doing the rounds, mostly among teenage girls. something heartbreaking about that, like the tremulous smiles and haunted eyes of all those "body-positive" posts. something watery and unconvincing. how there's a way of being exposed and imperfectly held, roughly handled, how you're not really anything. how your language isn't really anything but a crude stew, mostly bone, mostly air. in irish, *an lucht siúil*, or *the walking people*. how lovely says a lady at a reading, how *fascinating*. this heritage becomes a place for them to put their "magic": in literature, in film, how the other becomes a receptacle for past – and invented – enchantments, a way of both preserving and disowning the superstitions of long centuries. imagination makes a romance against which to measure you. and when you're not flamboyantly bohemian, reading fortunes in the palm of a hand, or hawking lucky heather on the high road , then you are not suffered to exist. irish "undesirables" joining roving bands of "gypsies". a counterfiet of a counterfeit. not even your own invention.

+

how lovely. borrow did this, and he's well named. george borrow: victorian novelist, ethnographer, and self-proclaimed "romany rye". fuck him. his highly romaticised fiction blurred with his ethnographic work to essentially create a discourse – as Hazel Marsh and others have noted – in which the "true romany" was continually held up against a miscellaneous tribe of impure itinerants; in which the "true romany" was defined by a particular constellation of attributes – attributes of which he himself was sole arbeiter – and in opposition to which he positioned other nomads, constructing them as degenerate, and therefore suspect and dangerous (wolves). miscegenation – that great victorian panic – between the "pure" romanies and these degenerate others produced threatening hybrids: "half and halfs" who initiated not only a biological degeneration but also a grand decline in language and in culture.[xix] borrow and his twisted ilk erected systems of classification to categorize romanies that were implicitly racist and hierarchical, zealously cementing the binary between the "real" romanies – defined as exotic, racially and culturally pure, uncontaminated and thus ahistorical – and assorted degenerate nomads – defined by cultural contamination, and subject to social and economic forces, their nomadism born of pressured necessity, not the product of a rich "oriental" tradition. mumpers, tramps. and some man bellows from the window of a white van: *hedge humping cunts!* that was a new one.

+

so what does it mean to be or not to be "white"? white is not a colour as such, which is why whit*eness* must define itself in relation to a sea of subaltern others; must strenuously perform itself against those others: through the overt violence of the military industrial complex, and the subtle, hidden violence of discourse. this performance is as visceral as petrol through a letterbox, as maddeningly nuanced as the law. whiteness is continually quantified and measured. this process is *so* continuous that white people have ceased to notice it at all. what's that sound? it's the ambient hum of presumed whiteness, the polite claquing of the implied white audience.

+

am i *sure*? and i think about the myth of "white fragility". it isn't merely that white people are seen as being more fragile, but that whiteness itself is a cipher for multiple forms of vulnerability, for a kind of desirable sickness. what we might call soft power, the power of softness. whiteness forms on the surface of power like the skin on hot milk. or, to put it another way, white fragility is money-men in gimp masks turned on by being whipped: it's a submissive pose, affording the luxury of surrender without conceding any real advantage. whiteness is a swooning tyrant in a gilded sickroom. it's an autocratic invalid. it's baby jane hudson throwing a tantrum.

+

my "sickness" is of the wrong order, as likely to lash out as to be *self*-destructive. it doesn't manifest in a languishing aestheticised weakness on instagram. it's awkward and unpleasant. to live and grow at the edge of society is to live and grow in conditions that are four times more likely to lead to severe mental health problems. but to live and grow on the edge of society makes diagnosis and treatment for these same problems extremely unlikely. instead you will be deemed "anti-social"; you will have "behaviour" and "impulse-control" issues, you will be expelled, ejected, eventually criminalised. either because *your* crisis, *your* vulnerability, *your* victimisation doesn't present as such, or because no one is willing to countenance that you might *be* victimised, vulnerable, or in crisis. i look around the room and i ask myself: how many of these people have ever been arrested? how many of these people have ever been in a fight? how many have ever punched walls or shop-lifted or scavenged or stole? how many have gone hungry? how many have known fear? real fear without exit or end? how many of them have ever been truly angry, flailing and raving and ridiculous with rage? i remember after thatcher died, and some smug shit on social media talking about how she didn't hate anyone, and that celebrating someone's – anyone's – death was grotesque and inhuman. that's us, then: grotesque and inhuman. to live without hate is either a luxury or a discipline. a luxury for those with power, and a discipline for those without. she had not been where our communities had been. or, if she had, she was trying to forget, was acting her amnesia, using her new-found "enlightenment" as a stick to beat us with. she performed her passive sickly-sweet whiteness, beaming it through the screen at us, for likes and likes and likes. facebook, as the new panopticon of moral correctness, magnified and refracted her whiteness, 'til it glared like the heat at the heart of the sun.

+

they prefer you dead, those people. by which i mean all those "sensitive" white middle-class students, ipodding winehouse or joy division, making a fetish out of music's doomed heroes because in their world doom itself is exceptional and exciting, so much so that it confers a kind of status. and being dead, these figures are freed from their difficult contexts, subsumed into a textureless meld with others superficially like themselves, where whiteness alone is the badge of their belonging: their exceptional, sensitive whiteness. the dead are safe, ready to be packaged, repackaged, re-written, written-over, claimed and reclaimed by discourse: there's a white middle-class discourse for every working-class subculture you care to name. mediation, intervention. the white middle class create the archive, the archive becomes the crypt.

+

am i *sure*? my head hurts. because their whiteness will not conceive or recognise another kind of whiteness. how they say "white working classes" in tones of hushed disgust. as if there are no white working classes, or the image is too monstrous to be admitted. "beyond the pale". do you know what the pale was? it was a strip of land that stretched from dundalk in louth to dalkey in dublin. during the late middle ages it was land in direct control of the english government. a pale is a stake or a fence or a boundary. "beyond the pale" is beyond the rule of law, beyond ordinary standards of morality or decency. it means *there be dragons, motherfucker*, there be catholics, and perverts and savages, oh my! the white skin is a border too, its purpose to repel and to contain. and i have transgressed, trespassed beyond the edges of this border into otherness. am i *sure* i'm white?

+

i am not their white, so i *must* be the white of their worst nightmares: a council estate "benefit queen"; some uncouth lump in leggings sponging off the state, no rounded vowels or self-control. child bride in fake tan; a wedding dress so heavy that it shreds my juvenile hips as i walk. the stuff of daytime television, their ugly copy-paste poverty porn. i slipped up, slipped out. they got a glimpse of "the real" me. someone asked me once if my family were like that family in *shameless*? or was my family more like the families in *big fat gypsy weddings*? the families in *bfgw* are not like the families in *bfgw*. *they* did this to them. this isn't who they are.

+

yes, i'm white. i am so glaringly white i am practically translucent. there is an irradiated, exorbitant quality to my whiteness: weird and unhealthy in ways that make a mockery of their fair skin. yes, i am sure. and i benefit from the mute assumption that i will sound and think like them. they are not *sure*. and they need to be sure. and the depth of their anxiety is frightening.

+

maybe they can tell they've pushed this too far. look at me like can't i take a joke? but i *am* the joke. and all my rejoinders taste of horse flesh.

OF FAMILIARS/ I SHALL GO INTO A HARE

this time it's true: no bourgeois *sozialer mord.* those *early and unnatural deaths* belong to you. fear us. fear us as you fear the crowd, the curse, the reeking incursions of disease. at the sight of us, your metaphors turn vermin. my dear *el presidente*, my dear elite, and all you fickle dreamboats of soft power, please. didn't you know? we spread by ripple and resonance – a rumour in your campaign prosodies. this time it's true: *evil* is *éveil,* to wake, arouse, to rouse, a ruse. ours is nightjar, nightjeer. jaw-jacked, jackdawed sky and us a swoon of birds, a sleeve of snakes. say us names: *malkin. vinegar tom.* sing *sack & sugar,* knit their wingspans into flight with fear. ours is cheap hashish and myrtle, myrrh's sweetest chervil murmur. attrition's stink. atonement's smoke. oracles of coronach: grief's gracious policy. knives jostle. our bladed laurels. adepts, nurses, we. thieves of thyme. of sorrel. of medlar's fuckpad mufti, the hedgerow's corpsy lore. we've hagtaper bullock's bane, a penny pricksong, lugs and worts. hey you, whoreson, sawbones, hawthorn suck. we're out for you. boil the bloodshot eyebright up, and sing us cunt a velvet thug. teased thread and bitten thumb. this time it's real. *all* of us witches. inflame your vacant stare with blutwurz, lobes of tormentil. tormented vessels burst. a bitter pill, a split lip, spill a saucer of sour milk. beat and fold a hex until it forms its stiff white peaks of s l o w poison. sloe gin. slurring low. *pyewacket & pigwiggen,* sing. *holt.* this halting site, this halting states. the man himself comes conjuredust and cortisone. silver thaler, cimaruta. talismen, us invisible friends. a kiss lands and a black spot blossoms. blots the sun. ours the incurable noose, the ducking stool, the stake, the brick through the window, the weight of a bull's balls swollen with blood, a letterbox gagging on petrol. anonymous hate-mail, and *all* of us witches. thin as a crease in a dirty sheet.

baby mama. scrape-backed ponytail, a whip without a hand. wiping a scream on your cheek. how a scream is a yawn with the sound turned up. we're tired of you, you sun-kissed kings of cancer, you courtesans of arcade fire and eye-fuck. us do the dryhump and the mandrake, and so many lovers. go blighted, lisping, stitch us shut. we trade in knots and scalps. slashed achilles, smithereens, moodswings, rings, miscarriages. in incantations, withering. call us *skadi*, scald-crow, backslang and axehead, the larynx crushed. the moon through all its deep throat phases, featherglide deluxe. we spit you back at you through the sewer of our saying. fatten the chattels, reprise your fire. it's real this time. we're with baba yaga. with pendle's tethers, the slings and arrows of islandmagee. we are with gowdie and chattox and dunbar. we are with lorde and with valerie solanas. we are with witches. all of us witches. the underworld attends us. buried at a crossroads, delivered to the compass, delivered of a rabbit, of a foreclosed farm, a ruined church. our slant and splitfoot operatives. their luckless delving rue. sieve the breath for nails. provocateurs: black calabash, black bowl, black drum. black bow, black hole, black gold. we know what we owe. the weeping yew, the slaughtered ewe, the warm embraceable you. watch us like an old maid playing patience, frail and sly. we peel our sleeves, reveal a ladder. we peel ourselves, revealed, reviled. this revelry, this reveille of skin. sing *elemanzer, peckin the crown*. drown, father-fucker. cat-shapes sit on babychests: *mačka*, the *marime*-most part of being. us straddle the bright air, piss standing up. where a foul mouth is a souvenir. the human ear, a heresy of pearls. teeth are strewn to hamper harvest. an errand out of ears of corn. sickened calves, a child entangled in a day-glo shriek. your parables and scams. fleece you, of all your moral fables, all your fabled marbles, all your summonses and psalms. oh, us from the mardy vagabondage of bog-places. read your red idea in dregs of cold tea. nettles and infection. *old time religion.* vestments and pedestals. girls gridlocked into girdles, lockstepped into marriage. oh herbicides, the common-law language of flowers, you heterofucks, you herods, you lordlings, your vocation of weeds. remedies, infections, a valkyrie solo for skinning a horse. the razor-tailed magpies. clockworked to conjuries of flight. glove the bone. chew the cud of burdock's false positive. hyssop swig and dittany. tansy, hellebore's ectopic slop. improvise our bridal rorschach one more time. hit us baby, one more time. impressionistic on our bed. the priests' collective guesswork wagging fingers over us. mess, corrective cleansing. whaleboned bursaries of flesh. the pumpkin splits. euphoria, the juices run and london's burning. keep your moon maidens, your swan maidens, soapy-soft and lyre-beguiled. oh, we're not *wiccan.* patchwork and craftfair and potpourri. women's work is gutting fish, whore-toil, endless pussy-craft. all of us witches. sprawling like a midland city. this body washes itself in the body. menstrual scum, ulterior honey, carpal sluts, all of us: rose-chafers, handmaidens, thai brides, bull dykes. the complete girlfriend experience. make scented forfeits from the sunshine. ribs like cattle grids, our eyebrows meet in the middle. we'll die. we'd rather die. than give an inch. defect. is the fault and the flight. fuck you. this be the night. fuck you.

MY ALTERNATIVE LECTURE ON FERAL
SUBJECTIVITIES

unaccustomed as i am to making speeches: anorexia as therianthropy. that is to say: life after rape. life after grief. that is to say: feral is a territory. no, that is to say: feral is not a state but a process. by which i mean – among other things – the melancholy *umwelt* of the queer. i shave my head. how feral is a gesture; the body without voice reduced to gesture. how gesture is both language and a failure of or substitute *for* language. to be hyper-visible, yet always somehow *missing*. what it means to be poor: the object of paranoid fantasies, scapegoated, caricatured, endlessly surveilled and administered. your existence hedged by legislation and bureaucracy at every turn. yet to figure in these systems as a problematic absence, imperfectly pinned down. there are *endless forms most beautiful*. how *other* multiples these sorrows: you are visible in all of the *wrong* ways; a target for ridicule and violence. you are a medical curiosity and a sideshow spectacle. you are inspiration-porn and a cackling cartoon baddy. you are a cautionary tale. you are a flag and a threat and an effigy made of yourself. your visibility is punitive, politicised and policed. you are supremely, dangerously *visible*, but rarely ever *seen*. you leave no wound, no trace. you are whispered into euphemism and dirty secret. you are papered over, painted out, redacted. yet *otherness* draws all eyes toward you. the only proof that you exist at all is the hostile regard to the crowd.

+

feral registers voicelessness, performs voicelessness, until feral is transmuted *into* voice, a way to express that which can never be said or refuses to be heard. did i say *feral*, i meant *hunger*, which usurps and *becomes* language; is both language *and* gesture. in ireland, the starving body functioned as both the emblem and the evidence of colonial oppression. a cipher of denial, of want, of articulate refusal. by which i mean the seanfhocail: is *fearr gaeilge bhriste ná béarla cliste*. what is the wasted body of a hunger striker, but *broken irish*? the self-evident scar of its mutilation? by which i mean that this body – this life – is mine, that i do not recognise your prison or the laws that it upholds.

+

feral doesn't want to die but to speak. feral must produce strange sounds or no sounds because the mouth is a nest for an enemy language. to talk "proper" what proceeds from us can never amount to more than a bargain basement version of our tormentors' voice. to speak without accent, to speak only through the mute grammars of negation. by refusing food, refusing their world. or else *let us howl*.

+

what i meant to say was this: what if feral were a method? what if feral were a method and a nectar? how language lives, is the medium and the object of our joy. to make more than the *kýrie*, than the *caoin*. feral lives in the desperate, suggestive part of language that is also the naebrained hormonal succulence of *fuck me!* of *get over here and fuck me like a red-headed step-child!* is a straggling, starloitered love between curfews, us hitching our tights in a tactical skirt. feral is not for *mean girls*. is for scavengers and synanthropes, never for predators. for those of us who, in the extrovert disastrophy of a secondary modern unmade ourselves. what i meant to say: feral is superbly adaptive. to exists under the shaping stress of a culture of a country that wants you dead, how that makes you not *resilient*, or *stoic*, but chimerical, mercurial, an impossible, incendiary form. in the needlenose night, you pass your tongue through a wishing ring twice, you nail your twilight to a tree, you step out of your skin. there are six dead crows poked with a stick, bent back on themselves like dismembered bibles. feral does not *endure* but *evolve*. the slangy taste of her name is tinned ravioli, and bread so thin that it lets in the light, is the rankled chests of children, penny sweets, where a sugar shrimp is a severed ear, where all the chocolate tastes like crime-scene chalk.

+

feral's gonna preach it like she feels it. is a *pleasure activist* in an era of long knives. to *activate* pleasure, in fact, and fuck their wheedling adultrip. feral says *screw your gym membership, your mortgage, your kitchen island*. what should cling to feral should be the promise and the solace of *escape*. to be *un*domesticated. to have *escaped* domestication. not the same thing. so feral is a choice, a refusal, a sensual refusal: she steps through the jaws of a corset to become – what? to be fecund with refusal. antigone's *no* without comment or apology, principled and vigilant, into the teeth of their feculent intent. how feral is a fuse, is insurrectionary fur. we should be feral, plotting joy's recourse through thorns, fishing for a song among the welter of our wounds. feral is *otkaznik*: those who are denied become those who refuse in their turn. feral is the unmutal ecstatic. is the five-hundred-and-umpteenth critique of oligarchy.

+

what if feral were rhubarb, grown from a seed in a bird-shite, its supple pong and sugar-dipped delicious bitter-sweet? my pinked teeth say this confectioners' error to stain. they say their stain. they say *what is a name but a trite condition of limit?* what is a country? what is a body? what is a home? feral should say: *what is form?* feral makes a mouth wide enough for lightbulbs. to *fix* her teeth is to equally bleach the language made in her mouth. a line of straight, white similes, the bland armaments of hygiene. feral's breath is bad, but her teeth are sharp.

+

men have emptied feral of all but fear and error, susurrus of dread, smarming from the gilded *sausage-fleisch* of a politician's tongue. what feral must find is the fluke of errant fairing. we can learn from those aerial truants, the gulls: oracles of unthought and amnesia, gulls, who mean and delight only in themselves. their feral bears no message. little worm, emissary of the ear, the air. feral knows a song that will get on your nerves. the animal without allegory. what i meant to say was: i spent that last four years as a hyena, turning my soft renunciate's muzzle to the wall. men will show you where her feral fails, those upright ingénieurs of fate and muck and standardised testing. a white hand caught in the warm folds of our otherness, washed in the weak heat of our warrens, our rookery blood. feral is like *queer*, cannot constitute itself: a perverse inversion of form, the squeamish miracle of desire – *contra naturam* – melancholy, melancholimost profane. men who say we have walked their rituals to widdershins, the body too, how we exceed ourselves, our sex, how we overstep our skin, how the wild will not contain us. edge incarnate, a circle without centre. the hyena's laugh is like the mona lisa's smile. no, not like: is.

what if feral were a tactic and strategy. to conceal and
to console, the wagging tongues of canting crews, the
spiegelschrift of evil twins. or what if feral were a girl? who
leapt from arrest into endless blue recidivist scrapyard dawns
no quarter given. not a *lovely thing*, not lyric's weary lilting,
lairy wilting, not any straying waif: impulse perfume, cheap
millennial flower crown, cheapest sateen pedigree and insoles
stripped from plimmies. there are men who bend god's speed
to their leering will. men are selling feral: as the gangrenous
atavism of a council estate. a foxy charm reworked as culling
law. where all tales tend to murder, where the drone of his
voice out-aria's any swarm. what if – ?

+

at the reading an actress hangs her heckle from a rounded
vowel, talks about *real people*. who are only ever scraped
from the pavement, who have no culture, only customs,
who's livid slang lights up the baccy night in strophes of
aggy verbal. my hyena is an elite of one, wants to say: *listen
fucker, our first language was trees, an alphabet too tall for
english mouths to mither, how they removed their teeth with
pliers, stretched themselves like snakes around the bonny of
it.* wants to say: *punch up, for once.* and *what about access?*
and *what about provision?* the muttering of currency. to be
all profit and no motive, you collaterals of tallow. england
has been shitting my figment flesh into fetish and rhetor and
feral forever. if we are not *real people* – ? that is: i fail to
belong even in the *other* you put me in. what if – ?

at the reading a poet tells me about the hyena's birth canal:
long, narrow, and with a sharp bend. over fifteen percent of
females die during their first birth. they lose sixty percent
of their firstborn young. why tell me this? is this what feral
holds? the freight of feral? who cannot even sex correctly,
whose cunt is a cold kiln, who cannot have children. will not.
whose body is an abortionist's closet. what if feral fought to
be here? in the queered time of the childless. has overcome
the stovetop cunning of grandmothers and all the *unwant*
of the church. feral as evidence, as a tactile fragment of sin.
but feral swims these reservoirs of foetal alcohol. how feral
is jugged in the chancy love of women. how feral will wear
her lips out in the wine. can feral *communion*? can feral *fruit
of thy womb*? a saint with a fragrant name. with a mane of
nuclear weather. tell a lie: a halo.

+

what if feral arrived, spoiling from a molotov, across the coaly
midland night, the mainland night, hymning all concussion's
protocols? *hyenas*, says the biologist, *bear a calloused clitoris*.
hyenas, he says, best all rubies, the eyes of idols, every belly-
dancer's jewel. what if feral were these thoughts, amplified,
exaggerated, where *animal* repeats: first as farce, and then as
pornography. how feral sees itself: in the muddy gape of a
wellington boot, a corpse's sleeve, a manual for processing
livestock. what i meant to say was: anthropocentrism isn't a
gift. you little us inside the human. and you little humans too.
what sentiment is is a turd wrapped in tinfoil masquerading
as the moon. my body is not a landscape, this landscape
is not a body. my body is not this animal. but i *am* every
animal, *it's all me-e-e-e!* all you single ladies, sing it now:

anytime you feel danger or fear, then instantly i will appear... you'd better believe it. feral is the opposite of *difference*, is the fear of difference, is the fear of feral, which you only know to crowbar, which you only know as a mechanism of eviction. what if feral weren't your *get thee hence*? what if feral stayed, will stay, and is? what i meant to say: oh queer ones, motherless daughters, the wolf-wombed, the womb-wounded. oh all my hyenas, we're coming, we're here.

LISTEN, FUCKER

'everything I love has come to me through English; my
hatred tortures me with love, my love with hate.'
– W. B. Yeats

'This is not a love song.' – Public Image Limited

what if i don't want to be consoled? or to console in my
turn? try to imagine anger as more than a *stage* or a *shtick*.
i will not *work through this* internally, politely repress and
appease with quiet dignity behind closed doors or in specially
sanctioned spaces. you want to draw a *cordon sanitaire*
between my dangerous rage and the world, and you keep on
asking me: *why are you so angry? lament* is not *elegy*. the
caoin carries both inconsolable loss and irreconcilable grief.
the *caoin* includes a call for vengeance, a reckoning with
the world. you keep your peaceable catharsis. it smacks of
absolution, it lets you off the hook. *feeling better* is a pretty
poor fucking substitute for radical action and organised social
change. i don't want to *cope* with an unacceptable reality, i
want to apply a vice-like pressure to those who engineered
it. i won't *write myself well*, idealise his dying *or* his life. i
won't dissolve the serial oppressions that beset us in some
vague gesture towards empathy, whereby the *beauty* of my
pain functions as a tacit justification for the inequalities that
produced it. listen fucker, that deep swell of feeling a poem
prompts may *seem* profound to you. may *seem* momentous
even. but it is interior, entirely subjective, the opposite of true
sympathy, true solidarity. this kind of poetry, and the idea
that it connects people through some golden thread of fellow
feeling conceals your responsibility for producing the wound.
you're a sly shit, you use catharsis to make a fetish out of

working-class *resilience*; you tie suffering to a marketable performance of identity, where our pain has meaning and value only in so far as it elicits a profound emotional response in our audience. where our pain has value so long as it only goes so far. don't challenge, don't change. i don't *want* to feel better. i want a world where nobody else has to die like that. i am the man of la mancha, my dream is impossible!

+

stage is both performance space and period of process. does that mean anything? how do you negotiate between the rage felt by an individual and the radical collective engagement such an individual demands? to elicit a sigh is an insult. to be required to mould our abject losses into readily accessible codes of plain statement is fucking offensive. the lyric has this instrumental eloquence, and the talking cure has it, and the whole world has it. you want an ideal of emotional expressiveness, but anger troubles identity, the normative performance of a *self* you think you know. anger unwoman's me, unenglish's me, it classes me until i'm werewolf and *hulk smash!* in my grief i inscribe the inequality that produced the trauma, the fatal extent of the difference between us: my carefully cultivated accent suffers slips, i run aground in my scuttiest clothes, i don't wash, i don't eat, i am wearing my postcode on *my face*, you say. at the reading after marty died, some woman *chav!*'s me. the more i try to keep my voice level and controlled, the more pronounced and unstable my accent becomes. at the end of the night the organiser corners me, tells me i was *unintelligible*, that i need to *enunciate*. he wears a microclimate of red wine fumes, a warm fug inseparable from his english, and i want him writhing in pain like a salted slug. he kept asking me where i was from, as if the way i sound must be continually explained or atoned for.

he felt he had the right: my vocal identity is inseperable from my status as a working-class woman, as an "other", and from the expectations that identity engenders. within literary space sound has a way of speaking to and through shifting perceptions of education and class, subverting or denouncing the political, social and poetic assumptions contained within notions of "accent" or "dialect". at an event that described itself as "experimental" and that celebrated the decentring of the lyric i, my strong vocal identity took a steaming shit on their much lauded "post-identity" poetic moment. they did not like that. and so i was raked over the coals for failing to modulate my class identity, and unsubtly mocked for the way my working-class body presented and took up space.

+

or say then, that i do not know *how* to talk: the passionate stutter, the indifferent slur. who cuts my tongue from me? belfast, *béal feirste*, a mouth subdued with sand, a fist is both the famine and the feast. but i am not *from* anywhere: how *both* has a way of being *neither*. no nation frames this, and all i have is english, to strive to starve without success to unmake the pain of english with english, to force the unhomely home to make room for me. *broken tongue.* i have all the words, but to speak english nicely and well is to compound the pain. how can language hope to provide a cure when it was instrumental in producing the wound? *terse*, someone says: to talk at the speed that paper tears, that coins are counted. i make animal sounds, the diaphragm frames this pain. this sound is all my knowing mirthless creoles, pidgins, cants. pigeons. birds, between *glance* and *grab*. say *state of grace* or better, the *grace of being stateless*. and they ask me: *why are you so angry?* they want me to smile, to speak in tepid villanelles about the self. they want a *story*. a *story* is a tune you can hum, is a plausible groove you can cum to. oracular: this fortune staggers tea-leaves, startles palms, subjects our utmost tender thought to a mercenary skinning. to a mercenary skin. to a mercy killing. i cannot reckon with this country anymore. give me shallow men of hospitable accord and light enough to see by. i will not insist. i will be gentle, content to be forced. i will not resist. i will not defend myself from flowers or from hearts. i will not ask permission or forgiveness. i will not ask for anything at all. who says that we have learnt to stick out our tongues? to stick out our hands? to whine in a wheedling quitter's lilt of benefits and banishments? this is *my* body, the immaculate national cabbage! if i carry it alone, will they love me? if i press it between pages? to the dead breath of revenue? i cannot talk. past-perfect daybreak, imploded bravado, a dead bird like a lost glove flattened to the road. mislaid a decade in the *waiting room*. it is the room that waits, not me. his mother says: *you've never always come from here, go back to where you're not.*

+

am i getting through? they sent me to see a woman with an office behind her eyes. *her* voice was process and audit. *her* voice was botched scientology. she says: *i know where you've been and i know where you're from.* and *her* voice was england's garden coast, its comely gloaming, cycle paths, historic piles. i don't know how to talk. i am making a me shaped hole with my mouth. that woman has skin like builder's tea, the morning a plausible roseate husk behind her. *people like you* she says, and she clots the mouth with a crocodile endearment. oh the lais, the lie, the mawkish entreaty, my own corroded pulse winding down in aertex rooms to cold grease and mildewed sublime. the humming sweetness of summer, radio voices like flies on fruit. *i* speak like the smashed mammal, pressing the raw disgrace of itself to the road, a hood without a head. and no i can't be *more specific.* a disorder of mood, a disorder of thought, *a derangement of the social senses.* i point out some sites of exorbitant malady: a baby's pink belly in the bathtub, my own thighs without tights, ants in a salad, a man in uniform. insomnia is being a small stone idol with agates for eyes. estates that smell like a stoner's cum sock, and i haven't slept since i began to name the things i saw. where the rainbow repeats itself, repeats on itself, where you can be a *victim* or else an empress of gothic humiliations in eyeliner on instagram. white alarmist faces peering through filtered portals, death masks cast in candyfloss. the rank breath of the long weekend, acute with the acetylene of self-love burning holes all over. i have no voice, a hurt i fit my face around. not shetland or in sunshine. not the mardy midland night where the theme is a sinister fury common to all. not in norn. not in tipp. the road as a leather belt you drag a razor down forever, marty said. to see yourself silently mouthing, small inside a dog's eye. you who have voices can not know what it is like to be so shrink-rayed. words you'll neither spit nor swallow, that dessicate while they preserve, like lye. the lie. the lie is mortar (masonry) and mortar (weapon). his name is unstable, is indirect fire. i'm attached to language by the weak grip of an undertaker's handshake. can you name the rock you crawled from? can you even name your name?

+

i say to the therapist: *what if i don't want to be consoled?* sleek and clean, step back into the world. what they call the world, the oblong box they put me in. and you fuckers, you can only understand language as a *way back*, as a yellow brick road and a pair of ruby slippers. worse, part retreat and part deliverance. mine is the "feral" menomic of collective fury. i want my words to burn the book that buries them; rage to exceed the scream that carries it.

WHAT IT IS

it is entirely possible to simultaneously benefit and suffer from the same set of assumptions. to put it another way: for the white other our privilege is also our pain. by which i mean subjective pain, systemic privilege. by which i mean we refuse to recognise our privilege because we are "hurt"; that we measure our subjective hurt against the systemic hurt of non-white "others" and pretend not to notice the difference.

+

by pain i mean those moments we wake in shock from the belief that our colleagues and peers regard us as equals. i mean the luxury of *being* shocked. we have entered the academy; we play out the pretence. we are somnambulists, amnesiacs, protected by forgetfulness, by daily acts of effortful dissociation. we "pass". we are adept at this, so much so that we convince even ourselves, and especially ourselves, and only ourselves. indeed, our deepest delusion is that anyone else is fooled. *it* begins, as it must, in the moments we run up against the real, in an endlessly iterative series of rude awakenings: but you don't *sound* working-class, oh, i didn't mean *you*, *you're* not like that; you don't *look* "gypsy". worse and better, we are told that we do not exist: either because the "class system" in england has ceased to exist, or because we are not a perfect fit for an imagined set of criteria, dreamt up by those who know shit all about us. we are *not* regarded as equal. the middle-class culture in which we find ourselves scarcely regards us as human at all. animal/ ghost.

+

i count the number of times tyson fury refers to himself as

an animal in interviews. or is referred to *as* an animal by others. it's a lot. i'm trying to write something about the ways in which working-class and "gypsy" discourses use both fear of animality and "concern" over animal welfare as opportunities to express and confirm a variety of shared class and racial hatreds; how these discourses are also constitutive of an ideal white performance: a refinement and generosity of sentiment towards "dumb beasts". nice ladies in hunter wellies with waxed barbour jackets scream at me about my "status symbol dogs", who bought from kennel club puppy farms designer animals so riddled with defects from inbreeding that their brief lives are a living hell of breathless torment. *my* dogs are mongrels and rescues and i love them with a fierce attachment i do not feel for most humans. i tell the nice ladies to fuck off and the phrase *you people!* is never far away. for my birthday a friend of mine buys me a jokey sign to hang on the office door: *never mind the pit bull, beware of the owner!* except she's crossed out 'owner' with a sharpie and substituted the word 'poet'. i'm aware that poet has become the polite word for 'pikey': a way of explaining the sharp edges of my identity.

+

the animal gnaws at me, the *idea* of the animal. it signals the too much, too present aspects of my identity. yet i am also missing. where missing*ness* adheres to me like a positive quality. i exceed and cross even the hodgepodge of stable categories that make up the chimera: an amalgam of known, possible, and impossible parts. i exist in a state of quantum uncertainty between less-than-material and more-than-natural. this has everything to do with class, but it is also about gender and sexuality, about being an unreliable receptacle for otherness. between and across. i am the interval. i am the cut.

+

strangers yell things at me on the street. they have been
yelling the same things at me since i was eight: are you a boy
or a girl? are you a man or a woman? these days i answer
them: *no*.

+

i am tenuous. thin. i *grasp* and i *stretch*, waltz with
the insubstantial stealth of shadows across your shit
commercialised scene-space singing: *what is the matter with
you?* straight people sit on the beach with their flags of
impossible country where pride is a picnic word you strain
through avocado halves, sagging in their cellophane, the
heart and its toxic praline. what i mean is rainbow capitalism
makes me want to vomit wasps. what i mean is fuck your
vinegar-stricken stomachs. heat. the sea is a sheeted mirror
this morning. boys, in the slapstick whims of attraction,
nerving themselves in a line along the front. those toiling
attempts at a kiss. some phantom darling, dilating their
dolorous strut up tontine street. youth, blousy, in the haywire
wanderlust of names. relics, accessories, heirlooms. eyes. the
man with leather haunches. the girl with her mouth cupping
the cold tit of an ice-cream cone. and the straight people sit
on the beach, in flip-flops and extrovert tolerance. children,
mawkish and mollified, oval faces swollen with too-much-
sun. *what is wrong with me?* the tongue is an enemy tenant
i struggle to evict. how i want a sky, inflated with thunder.
how i want the pumpkin pull of an orange moon. old women
rise, nervous and offended, flee to tiny bungalows made
sinister with knitting, composing their dusty exemptions

from carnival. what is it that the past says in its gramophone vernacular? *faggot? queer? sordinn? bull dyke? lesbo? argri konu?* i will close my door, the shellac's *aisteach* suctions for company. my box of bleached mementos: her vivid face, pallid with harassment. she broke her sprawl against stone. industrial towns intoning shame. where the straight people sat on the beach. where their do nothing died on their lips before skinheads. what i mean is a sticker that says: *not the fun kind of queer*. what i mean is desire transforms the body, and abject desire makes the body abject. what i mean is weasel, hyena, hare.

+

all of which to say i am reading judith butler while crying: identities 'are never fully or finally made; they are incessantly reconstituted, and, as such, are subject to the volatile logic of iterability.'[xx] i am talking about "passing". i am talking about the privilege and the shame of "passing." i am talking about the ways in which class, ethnicity and sexuality mirror and problematise each other within cycles of concealment and disclosure. i am talking about the profound instrumentality of "passing", and the fear that incubates inside of it. i'm talking about the ways i cancel myself out.

+

another day, another essay. there are statistics; there are well-meaning surveys. there is evidence. but evidence of what? when i look for our lives i find myself reading the spaces between the words, attuned to silence, stutter, lack or gap; to what's omitted or erased, all the little deficits of data that contrive to lose a life. and you want to scream: *here i am, i am real!* but how do you prove a negative? we have visibility, neoliberal culture insists upon that. it claims that visibility is synonymous with voice, and an adequate substitute *for* it. it's not. i want to talk about his death. i want to talk about suicide. i can read that some 92% of travellers hold no qualifications equivalent to or higher than gcses; that levels of non-attendance at secondary school are high, and at tertiary level practically non-existent. can read that adult literacy among traveller communities is a shocking 10-15%. or that only 11% of traveller men of working age are in full-time employment, that the life-expectancy in traveller communities is 11-15 years lower than the national average. what does that *mean*? the faint distorted traces of those whose only language is loss. these statistics inscribe inferiority, they mark a transition from *person* to *problem* with the apparatus, language and collective imagination of the state. these statistics erase persons, and yet they also bind them, to an image of themselves as characterised by failure, deficiency and want. reports intended to provoke action or secure aid end by disappearing those whose existence they purport to signify. all that appears is plight and naked need: the open mouth, the empty hand, until the human sinks into stereotype and vanishes without a trace.

+

that, or we finish as a crutch for white supremacy. because when we are not degenerates, we are victims, in both popular and political discourse. we're a structural rebuttal: they point at us and say "white people are suffering too" as if that's the clincher. they don't give a shit about us the rest of the time, but they'll wheel us out and dust us off when they need to. they say, "look at how much the *white* kids are struggling", "look at all these *white* kids, left behind", as if that were the fault of minoritised groups and their advocates. how does it feel to know you're a spanner in the works of any progressive reform with race, gender or disability equality as its focus? not great, but "white but not quite" props up this institutionally racist shit-baggery, with or without our consent.

+

we are all schrödinger's fucking poor people: called into being by political expediency. the rest of the time we do not exist. no would deny that *poverty* exists; everyone is quite prepared to perform distress at the existence of *poverty*. it is a terrible thing, but it is always happening elsewhere, to an idealised victim who bears no resemblance to you. worse, for many members of the middle-class poverty, itself becomes a kind of inscription surface, an aestheticised stele, a depthless backdrop. the poor and working-class people who negotiate and inhabit this poverty are always missing. the social forces that create and contour the experience of *living* in poverty are excised so that we flicker across this backdrop in vague and fitful gestures, empty tropes. and if you deny the existence of the poor, then poverty is empty and up for grabs. this is an integral part of the mechanism by which gentrification operates: class is refused in the very instance it is enacted. the middle-class talk endlessly about "regenerating deprived areas". areas are not "deprived", fuckwit, people are. the human is edged out of language as a precursor to being edged out of civic space. they arrive in our communities — attracted precisely by the frisson of glamour, the cultural cache, the *aura* that surrounds poverty— and they begin living life without any responsibility or reference to those their presence has impacted and displaced. they don't ask themselves where we go to. they see florists and boutique bakeries flourishing around them and they are well pleased. they walk through people as if we were not there. this is transmitted and enforced through culture. the middle class has been so effectively naturalised as the sole implied audience for art and literature that they feel no qualms about using their own experience of the world as an absolute model for all human experience. as with the idiotic toby young claiming that the ken loach film *i, daniel blake*, didn't "ring true", middle-class illusions persistently carry more weight than our poor or working-class reality.

+

frequently, we are not trusted to be the authors of or experts in our own experience. when we are allowed to contribute to culture, through our art and writing, our subjects are assumed to have a moral obligation to be "inspirational" or "heroic" according to the arbitrary standard of a culture we cannot access or participate in. to the middle-classes an "inspirational" subject can only ever be one who "transcends" the socioeconomic conditions into which they were born. they welcome only work that endorses the belief that this is possible. further, they refuse to credit any other kinds of "success", or to understand that the working class may not want what they want. they refuse, absolutely, to recognise their own desires as subjective and contingent. they *are* the world.

+

and so we are often unsure of ourselves. we live without certainty, never knowing where we belong and what belongs to us, our right to take up space, the parameters of the possible, the contours and dynamics of any social situation. most days we feel small, unsure and dirty. inside the academy, within art and literature, in "elite" cultural space, and in department stores or restaurants, in gp surgeries, at dwp appointments and at job interviews. i used to think that there were so many rules and i could never master them all, but that's not quite right. the "rules" are for us "others". white middle-class people don't develop a sense of certainty from knowing, but from never actually *having* to know. *any*thing. about *any* situation. they can make assumptions about their rights, their welcome, their dominant knowledge. they can expect to go unchallenged, or challenged in such a way as to further the reciprocal work of their superiority—conferences, for example, all those gracious, musing interjections, their deference to the assumed expertise of the other like themselves—they don't need to connect agency and status, that's the power they have. and when this certainty stalls or stutters, then it recuperates that agency, that infernal fucking momentum, by staging its own ignorance as badge of honour, as a bravura performance of "curiosity", making you the ambassador-apologist for your culture or community, expecting that their demands for information and enlightenment will be met by someone else. this whiteness is the self-effacing abdication from the work of knowing.

+

but shit, have i not flirted with this too? have i not hidden my fear because i can? have i not brazened it out and benefited from that assumption that i am like them? perhaps all whiteness is this same kind of squirming self-protection. what if whiteness is not an identity any more than white is a colour? what if whiteness is a strategy, a tactic, for securing and preserving privilege at any cost?

back in workshop land, and mr s. double-barrel asks me "what is that? is that supposed to be latin?" *it's shelta.* two unspoken assumptions here: that it is the classical allusion alone that is proper to poetry, and that my attempted use of any such allusion will be ill-advised and certainly defective. otherwise, why not simply ask me "where's that from?" or "what does that mean?" at best, the moment serves to expose something about the set of cultural expectations that colour middle-class engagement with poetic texts. at worst, it's a nod toward my not-belonging: not that i'm necessarily *unfamiliar* with ancient latin sources, but that someone like me cannot be trusted to handle them "correctly": i'll whack them in just any old where, misspelled, misapplied, and out of context. i profane the language through my use of it. my brain flashes up: wagner! who didn't want jews listening to his music in fear that this would retroactively taint his work. as if listening had such power, as if culture were so brittle. this is a kind of "white fragility" transferred to the art made by whites; an autocratic insistence on the unsullied purity of a dominant culture; a dominant culture taking refuge in virginal weakness. i frown. i repeat.: *it's shelta.* pause. "what's that?" in an accusatory tone. it's not that he doesn't know that irritates me, it's precisely that tone, embattled, bristling: his ignorance is *my* responsibility, *my* problem, *my* fault; that this textual "otherness" is purposefully alienating him, that he is the implied audience for *all* printed media and that i therefore have to manage and package my "otherness" for his comfort and convenience. somebody suggests i should provide a glossary, or footnotes. *or you could just google it?* they pile on, telling me that it jars, that they don't know how to pronounce the words, that they're disruptive "to the rhythm", that the lines require "context" to "help the reader along". what reader? whose rhythm? as if iambic pentameter were the only game in town. and had it ever occurred to anybody that "disruptive" might be the point? a debate ensues, about the uses of epigraph and allusion, the kinds of claims they are making for the poem and the poet, but also – to my mind anyway – how they often function as a kind of class-based coterie address that automatically excludes anyone without the wherewithal to recognise or decode them. picture a snobby bistro that posts up its menus in french: there's a seeking of prestige and a confirmation of status in knowing. and those who don't are scared off: *this is not for you.* but the white middle-classes can go "slumming it" any time they choose. they believe – and they believe because they are so often confirmed in this belief – that everything is *for* them. because they refuse to credit the complex intellectual, aesthetic and rhetorical roots of our language, art, and culture, they feel confident that they can ape our codes of behaviour and speech; can trespass in our world with ease. whenever they like. we are not aware enough to notice, or, if we do notice, why should we not be charmed and delighted by their condescension? mr s. double-barrel doesn't like my shelta because the shelta says: *no, this is not for you, you do not belong here. there is knowledge here you don't just get to skim or skate over. if you want this, you have to confront, reckon, stay with, make an effort.* effort is required, which is something that seems not to have occurred to many of these fuckers before. this can't just be copied, troped, assimilated and spat back out. it's not an over-priced van on the south bank serving mexican "street food". it's not a shitty shoreditch bar calling itself favela chic. i'm "ranting" now, because i'm feeling this. i say: *would you be talking about glossaries and footnotes and alienating my audience if i wasn't white?*

+

"you can't say that!" a woman shrieks. she misses the point. chiefly that one of the unique joys of being a "white, other" is that you present an opportunity for nice, white middle-class people to comfortably indulge both their racism and their classism without ever having to admit to the existence of either. they don't see your class because you do not present to them like a "typical" working-class person according to the tropes they themselves invented, or because they do not believe the class system exists at all. they filter class out of their world-view in ways that remove the experience of class-based oppression from black and minority ethnic people, while refusing to acknowledge the roll racism plays in the perception and treatment of white, working-class "others". they can make the fatuous statement: "but there are no working classes any more" because they don't allow themselves to see – to paraphrase the poet martin hayes – the thai manicurist or the ghanaian road sweeper as members of an oppressed class cohort.[xxi] in a similar but opposite way they project their own class privilege onto those with whom they share a superficially similar racial profile, so that *all* white people are, by their logic, an undifferentiated middle-class. to avert to this is, by a perverse distortion of logic, to be considered racist. in the workshop, discussion descends into an orgiastic performance of white guilt.

+

i don't mean to deploy the phrase "white guilt" in the way it is so often deployed: as an accusation or a put-down, designed to conflate an amorphous shame at *being* white with the specific and historical guilt felt *by* "whites" in order to present both as equally interior and baseless. i mean to describe an emotion predominantly felt by middle-class people. in my more cynical moments, i mean to describe an emotion more performed than felt. by which i mean, the performance of "white guilt" becomes part of the performance from which a certain kind of desirable "whiteness" is constituted. by which i mean that fomenting and policing class distinctions between white communities has become a key tactic for evading responsibility for racism. in the first instance, middle-class people blame "poor white trash" or "chavs" or "pikeys" for racism. in the second, we "pikeys" are shamed for our failure to live up to our "whiteness". again, we are dirty and uncouth, and stupid and mean. because of our inability to behave in accordance with white social etiquette, we blur the imagined boundary between white and non-white people. a profession of "guilt" is part of the performance from which a "good" or "worthy" white identity is composed. a contradiction emerges: they are superior because they advocate for racial equality, they are engaged in a public and collective discourse of a white moral reckoning; yet we are *inferior*, aligned with those racialised "others" because we cannot or will not tow an imaginary white line. it is so tangled. but fundamentally racism is *not* a moral dilemma. it is institutional, social, political, and historical. it's not about your warm fuzzies. racism doesn't care that you're a "good" person.

+

as a queer person from a marginal working-class background, i'm obscurely aware i'm supposed to feel grateful for the "rescue" afforded me by the lovely, tolerant middle-classes, and that anything less is mauling the hand that feeds me. i am also supposed to celebrate my every success as emblematic of and metonymic for the triumph of "my people". but i refuse to endorse this fiction. winning an industry prize is enormously gratifying, but it doesn't do shit for anybody else. they can't have it both ways: either my life was so terrible that it demanded escape into this aspirational paradise in order for me to "realise my dreams", or else neoliberal culture itself becomes the enlightened saviour, custodian and champion of that life, those lives, those dreams. this kind of cake-and-eat-it position requires "my people" to be – simultaneously – bigoted fuckwad lumpen-proles and the unfeasibly valorous victims of a natural disaster known as "inequality". they can use the word "inequality" without once alluding to the persons who benefit from, enforce and maintain it. i am a firm believer in the teleological argument for the existence of elites: poverty exhibits intelligent though malignant purpose and design. it is done to us by others, deliberately. and it is poverty that creates a vulnerable underclass of others – over-policed though under-protected – and the social conditions in which we *become* vulnerable.

+

i have *reclaimed* glissant *for white discourse*. when i am told this i cannot stop crying. i cry often lately. i am also dimly aware that – in a certain sense – my tears are the function and the badge of my privilege, my passing. retreat into weakness when the act fails. it's self-indulgent. i dislike myself for it. but at least i don't let her see me cry. never show weakness. not ever. that's their schtick. cry in the bathroom. smother my sobs in a stack of paper towels. i was trying to explain: how *opacity* exposes the limits of representation. that is, a gorgeous unquantifiable alterity, a diversity that exceeds any category imposed upon it; resists those poisonous hierarchies of absolute othering. fuck any cohesive and totalising claims of *identity*. i wanted to honour and celebrate this work of resistance, and i wanted to talk about the urgency of any poetics that has these flights of evasion and fugivity at their heart. i wanted to talk about shockley and mullen and smith, how their poetries reinvigorate and sensitise critique of the lyric self, and how much this had meant to me. i did not intend to trespass. i meant only to connect. *opacity* could be shelta too. *opacity* takes a language frequently described as less a language than a tactic, and makes it silver, makes it sing. and yes, *tactical*, but also radical, imaginative and controlled. that *opacity* becomes both a critical and a generative tool, that i am trying to perform shelta's varied escapes and feints by making both a mode and a commentary of evasion. within the space of the poem the survival strategies of historic traveller and working-class communities are reconfigured as tools for destabilising or reinventing poetic method. this is a work of love. what to do when any cohesive sense of identity has been disrupted by trauma? when your identity and the coerced accounting for that identity forms the *basis* of that trauma? when you live within institutional imagination as congenitally criminal, subaltern, or otherwise defective? love. and calling into question the implied ethical imperative contained within the claims of neoliberal identity politics to visibility as an exemplary political platform. the right to be *un*seen. the right to reticence. to question the ways in which visibility is compelled by discourse and by the apparatus of the state. because anti-trespass laws. because priti patel and legislative cleansing. because dale farm and smithy fen. because endless evictions and *big fat gypsy weddings* and the woman who said "we've a pain on our shoulders from carrying coffins". where is the white discourse that can hold this? for all my vanished others, my lovely stupid dead best friend.

+

i go running. as i run i repeat: *but, having naught, i never feel alone/ and cannot use another's as my own.* i have been on trespass in my walk today. but where is *my* discourse? when i try to write and think like them, there are "gaping holes" and "worrying gaps" and clumsy repetitions. will white always make attempts at solidarity de facto acts of conquest? or maybe it's something else. like the way political centrists use the rhetorical frameworks of identity politics to take-down left-leaning opponents. specifically – as shannon sullivan points out in *good white people: the problem with middle-class white anti-racism* – how clinton-biden represented the sanders campaign for democratic leadership as an anachronistic class-war agenda that deflected attention from white racism, an act of moral noise making that wilfully ignored one glaringly obvious fact: that class inequality is an inherent and structural feature of fucking racism; that racism is an inherent and structural feature of class inequality.[xxii] in the uk there are definite parallels within labour's endless "anti-semetic" witch hunt. in both cases accusations of racism against other others are used to derail any kind of systemic challenge, and to elide acts of class-based oppression. in *white discourse* i'm yoked to other white persons in ways that elide our difference, and my context. it isn't acknowledged that there are categories of *white* who are also excluded from whit*eness*. because we're white, we're the same. it's not that there isn't difficulty. so glissant is not *for* me. i get that. the pain felt by the white other is different and less; i benefit from this imaginative yoking even as it causes me pain. but am i really failing in my gratitude, care, or responsibility to the colonized other? or am i failing again in my white performance? the endless tedious maintenance of boundary and binary.

because denial of the inequalities produced by capitalism is absolute within neoliberal culture, and because an understanding of class dynamics is removed from any reading of ourselves, our lives, or indeed our art, we appear to the middle classes as – at best – incomprehensible and, as cynthia cruz puts it, 'enigmatic', or – at worst – chaotic, disordered, directionless, threatening. they cannot understand our motivations or behaviours in terms of class; they do not understand the social forces that contour and compress every aspect of our lives, and so they ignore and erase difference, or they invent reasons of their own; they project, fabricate and overwrite. that's power. that's real power. it's the power that 'other' removes from 'white', how 'other' denies and cancels 'white', how the forward slash performs the divide between 'white' and 'other', self and self. in the workshop they hear my comment as a denial of black pain, as a petulant *what-about-me?* but it's not. there's the systemic pain that is inscribed across and enacted through insurmountable and explicit difference, and the subjective pain of invisible othering. hierarchy is expressed through the refusal of this pain too. what right have you to complain? aren't *you* one of us after all? one of us when it suits us to see you so. one of us when belonging invalidates your grievance. your grief.

THE ACADEMY AS HIGH SCHOOL/ ATTEMPTS AT
MEAN GIRLS

the fuck is this? in a clique-work wasteland, girls. stereotyped in ways not smart. there's a burning book. kids enticed into animal overthrow. boys whose theft is an incomplete thrill. *losers! skanks!* and a charmed life aping shame. homeschool kid, your face a clueless moon on your first day, and on all days hereafter. i am a passenger, *you* are my puppet. in cubicles glitch an elliptical wrath. the eardrum bursts, attempting to bury these buds in our skull. dead-eyed. insensate with melody. the girl whose hair is a rumour mill, the mythical shockwave of puberty. poisonous, polarizing blondes. to persist in an idiot town wear a bulletproof pink. where pink is a *sieg heil!* the girl is outrageously famous. she has such white teeth. no poetry is ever getting past them. make a bonfire of your vetoed math. the lie travels through so many mouths on its way to you, it is cud by the time it arrives. refuse to hear. make your heart a portable columbine. that girl is an axe wound. that girl is an axe in heat.

+

sometimes i dream about it. the hysterical hum of a secret shared. i set a riot van on fire. i smacked that cop. but my heart is a cream-coloured sample-sized soap. i can't walk past a group of *gadje* girls, even now. bad nights, where reason reshapes my knuckles against the glass. the disintegrating body, disgusting to itself. there's a *slut rule*, a zombie bride, a devastating playlist. besties, a silky little ditto, and a phonecall to fugly. *the fuck is this?* killing flies in multiples of iridescent dispatch. each fly has the face of a girl: the girl who made me drink her spit, the girl who smeared shit on my chair, the girl who took my towel so i would have to walk home wet, the girls who followed me everywhere, who wrote me on the walls, the girls who called me *terrorist*, the girls who had their boyfriends hold me down, who ducked me under water, the girl who – years later – tried to make her guilt my problem. fatherfucker, i measured my brokenness out in dogs to a losing theme for decades. fear is a trickle of discharge, the suicidal fact. you don't know what you did. ancestral curses meet in the mouth, and i was too on fire to function. i mean too gay. in school death is a *yo!* that dress is the sickest burn yet, and all joking aside, in the silence of the bed i can hear my bodyhair thickening. i become a black rug on which you wipe your feet. like all my people. where are the poor kids in this film? where are the solitaries, ready to stab you in a feverish whisper? i'm doing the sequel. the vengeful ghost of valerie solanas is directing. there will be no cathartic tiara, there will be no circle of trust. cady as carrie on purpose. the pig is the prom date. the pig is a palace. the worst musk wafts from her. she owns it. *scarlet ribbons for her hair.*

+

regina george is too much morning. i mean, she reminds me of life, my viva, this meeting. women, this school is their paris and that's just sad. of course they know the difference between *garments* and *clothes*. of course their internal organs have been replaced with crystal slippers. and of course there's a silk corsage where their hearts should be. but still. their world is a tiny hell enclosed inside a pendant, they have issues rather than feelings. when they die the body comes back as bitches, as lilac spiders. they inherit the sun, them and their forcible cunts forever. yes, they have doctorates. being clever is another kind of theft, another kind of weapon. when they gaze at you, they stare through lavender cataracts, everything hazy and pretty and small. they have male secretaries and women to clean their kitchens. an opinion is an accessory too. carefully *queer* in a footnote font. sex without error, imperishable type. they live off overpriced salad, recycled hype, and our insecurities. regina george never dies. she goes from town to town with the school on her back. she is legion. everywhere you'll find her, tank-tops on tuesdays, consecrating incense to her self.

MEDITATIONS ON THE LIFE AND EXAMPLE OF SAINT VALERIE

call me a witch, i will show you a witch. i am half pharaoh and half corpse. that is, all woman. through the drugged attrition of late adolescence, with a limp calm, dressing for breakfast.

+

at the funeral, offering our condolences in a psychopath-test falsetto. we cannot wait to talk about ourselves. my father, vivisected splendidly, the weight of a white shadow.

+

at school i borrow the head of a horse. i want to be *beautiful*, anaemic and gaudy. my most languid disguise is a cat with a pastel paw. in the dream i am injured, anointed. wastrels wearing flower crowns strew my path with roses.

+

the man moving over me in macabre eclipse, his lips dropping insolent valentines. assailant, assassin, all his footsteps are addressed to me. the mind and its buried devils. the girls and their scrupulous malice, populist and absolute. in the medieval poem the names of the hare, the hare has seventy-seven names. i have seventy-seven names, and a burlesque of bad luck the same.

+

my sonnet is a suitcase, inexpertly packed: crinolines, ox-bloods, superfluous tulips, the aubade, the dirge, all

admonition's carnival. my poetry is like vodka, tastes only
of itself.

+

i was set adrift on a bamboo raft under a rose-pink sky. i
put the conch shell to my lips and bugled a reveille.

+

at seven, intently beheaded, val is her own stubborn double.
a child counts roses on the swing seat. she remembers the
gum in her hair.

+

let's not be *those* women, falling apart in fine regency
fragments. a white dress is pretending you're dead. a white
dress thinks it's better than you. this is called *fetish capital*.

+

take to your bed, buying star-fucker sandals on sale. cry
for days, learn how to account for flowers, domestic gin,
get real *classical* about it. stand around in fountains, your
mouth all smooth with rumour, do *la dolce vita*. incur a
saint's displeasure.

+

in the future there is tentacle-sex, nectar from another
daughter's tongue, the alienation of labour. if she loves you,
she will love you forever and ache you to the light. more likely,
she will not love you. a shut mouth leaking its blank unsaid.

couldn't wait to comb the church from my hair, blessing
myself by black gloves and patent moons, by holy salt. girls,
all flesh and fleece. there were morgues, mirrors, intended
smoke.

+

a flame in the lightbulb abodes of the skull is wagging, is
waging a merciless halo. later, you may find yourself bruised
by the cyborg blade of her tongue. she delivers and resists
all names. she cleans the names, the knives that cut the
names from culture. look out! it's feeding time at the zoo.

+

    antagonist, fur collects on her tendons.
    fur collects in her cells. she is changing.

+

men are a fleshy back in bed. he has no edges, no accent.
he is a sponge, a screen. if she can't use words, she will say
it with squirming, or an *i want* loop, or a lobbed bottle of
boiling piss.

+

better dykily psychotic, than a soother, a breeder, an ego
booster. because they tried to pay her in peaches, 'cause they
said their pretend at the protest. 'cause they called her a
saint but they kept the receipts. *abused crack-pot*, her brain
a round window, a perfect, disposable 'O'.

+

she signed her name as string of pearls. these robbery thoughts
her own. vandal, a skin stitched into miracle. each womb a
needless prison, each daughter receives a needless wound.

+

we will never be as full as they are empty. cities do their
fibre-optic amen underground. worms are perverts and
they get in everywhere. contaminants, inferiors, better to be
dead. we asked valerie for guidance: her head was a lantern
in a lion's mouth, inspecting error.

FOR BRITNEY
(OR WHOEVER)

throw him in the cellar, full grown. touch him, with a coy and rationing love among roots. nights spent stroking a mortal sin like a persian cat. the heart *wants what it wants,* is a godless baby monitor. ingénues eaten like eels, their cold stock becoming jelly. now is the winter of our hell-debut, our velveteen paedo in boudoir shock, our medicated sacrament. sleep to impress, simulate coma. be a briar rose, a fuckable brer rabbit. or be a shrewd pony. throw him to the floor. *we* chose pale hands and projects, the merlot of allotted suffering. listen: see by the light of a slight boy, skin like a catalogue onesie, peel his lingering peach from him. i won't argue with you. with *what big teeth,* and forget about oz. *this* is the world. valerie, saint valerie, cephalophore, her voice inside a nightlight, listen: *you'd better cut them up before they cut you down.* sister insider, why are you crying? the crêpe de chine of a normative lullaby.

+

put it this way: lives can begin past ringlets, in a grownup speech, completely at pen with yourself. deep in a different dress. deep in the outline of an animal. recover the lost symmetry of seizure. become a hyena, a skin stitched from expiry. amplify your razorblade virginity. the martyr is also the murderess. wearing the night-vision goggles of absolute rage. tempestuous and hirsute, find him where he lives, in a final tomcat shroud, and show no mercy. flow into foxholes and bunkers in a gown of sour gasoline, in a skirt as sheer as your stride, in a see-through stocking of napalm kirsch. you are made of moths, eat into him. a virus of light, you are the stuff of versace. leave him travestied and gutshot, straight to fucking video. don't be afraid. you fit him like a shiv. these steel toe boots are a double permission. trample a vera wang carpet of roses. until he is inside you, and not in a fun way, thrashing and submerged.

+

i'm not going to tell you you are beautiful. no one is. get over it. the beauty is over. is there life after life after years of dickless wonders screaming through the winding sheets of unexceptional privilege? is there life after *mad bitch* and hatemail, risperidone side-effects? yes, and no. i mean yes, but it doesn't look like you. stop trying. and know you were never more warrior. that feral girl saved you, refusing their puritan rooms, their sunday distinctions. *getting well* doesn't mean *going back*. don't be a pink plastic witness, a molested doll, a *rose* upstairs. don't collect in their cameras like sand. like sighs. now you are the size of yourself, be the size of yourself. *sane* is a model prisoner. *lovely* is the blue weatherproof uniform they'll leave you to die in. listen: be a hyena. the four of clubs is a witches' card. you've no need now for their catwalks or closets, their nonchalant incest, their hoaxes and frauds. it's a bad erotica, the opposite of stars. you *know* what it's like to be naked: a swaggering nemesis, the rorschach stain of complete despair. when they *don't know what to do with you, you've won.* your smile a teasing chemtrail, troubling the ozone, your marketable face.

+

there we were in mind-control-sized pieces. variant blondes, goosebumped décolleté and slouched. narcissists and gargoyles, the same obedient female as always. our outfit was nothing but nipples. our eyes do the dead-sea-saunter over stones, through sea-estates, undine undone, through chattering teeth, a recession of salt. discreet mermaids. dainty phantoms. how miserable a thing, ecstatic cage of fame. lady, make an asset of your faults. the body pushed to a corporeal exit. psychological vomit, self-help, candy and assault. let's be real here: drown him. in swimteam tendrils, the comfortless suck. absorb him. take him in through the fine amphibious skin of celebrity. or live to see your meatiest fails become memes. palming a face with a fucking brick. drown him, them, then return to hyena, sweet tooth forsaking marzipan. a torn throat always. come, bring your fat thighs and sorely debauched animus. don't strike a pose, strike a match. be the negative of lust. no one is looking, and you've been a ladder, frankly. we all have. consider the body: a rose garden, a traffic accident, a self-portrait in medical beige. screaming in garbled jurassic outbursts, pull the flowers from your mouth, rip your hair out at the root. change. god is dead, eaten by lions. is lions eaten by lions.

say this, then: as a "white other" i inhabit a cultural world that simultaneously provokes response and silences reply. which is pretty wearing. and what to do with this voided tongue, these affects without expression? i will tell you what i mean: i read a nauseating article, which dwelt upon the "enchantment" and the "mystery" of circus and fairground; of "gypsy" encampments and other such "liminal" spaces. not being the implied audience for this text, and having no access to the elite publication arena in which the article appeared, i found zero zone of response, no place of reply or respite from the cold rolling waves of fury that the work initiated in me. i knew the author, slightly. which somehow served to shake my confidence in even my own anger. who am *i* to question? who am *i* to challenge? where would i put this? and what would be the result? don't talk to me about social media. twitter is cú chulainn fighting the sea: it eats your rage and spreads it thin across the fitful continuum of collective attention. that is not a reply. at best it is an echo without origin. you become noise, a distraction, interference. the culture war absorbs you, recycles your rage into disembodied content. what is rage without a body? rhetoric. an acousmatic fart in a jar. i could craft a reply for the one journal that reliably publishes my prose. i could edit, send it somewhere else, somewhere new, but in order to do that i would first need to clean myself up, write myself out of my own anger. i could be visible. i could even be heard. but the voice that reached my auditors could never be my own.

+

now when i'm asked if i'm writing a book i tell people i am embracing the rant as a native art form. native to where?

the independent people's republic of feral children. if pushed
– although i'm rarely pushed these days – i say that i am
no longer interested in writing my monograph, in attending
workshops, running workshops, speaking at conferences or
submitting my writing to peer review. i pre-empt my own
rejection and console myself with the absolute license of
unfettered fury.

+

the author of that piece: i will never match her weight or
her reach. authority and status are encoded into her every
pronouncement, her every digital gesture. we could both be
described as "early career academics" as far as that goes; we
are both published poets, but i am neither young or pretty. i
don't breathe the same air. i've had dirty hands and broken
nails since the day i was born. it has taken me longer and cost
me more to arrive at a less-good version of the same place.
she is middle-class.

+

when the author writes about the margins, they are, for
her, devoid of context, of the class dynamics that created
them, and so they become a mirror, or a hollow repository
for her awe and sense of spectacle. in the process she erases
the real people who occupy those margins, and who have
not the opportunity or ability to reply. as she erases them,
she also imbues them with a silent and fascinating power.
that power is the pull of her "enchantment". how to say,
that essay emptied the margins, evicted me from the one
place i felt entitled to exist. all i could do was to push back
with my own cancelled voice, as if the author could hear,

as if she were listening, as if the voices of people like me counted for anything, registered on the recorder, were not indistinguishable from background fucking static.

+

so i say with a voice that is the negative of voice, that enchantment is also a function of privilege. enchantment implies an edge, and an edge presupposes a limit, so she says to herself *i will go no further*, and she goes no further. the limit is the end of the illusion, it is also the beginning of the threat. on the threshold – more *threshed* than *held* – in the tiny dwellings among the washing and the weeds, *mystery* is a willed failure of imagination, a refusal of life in all its smallness and mundanity. objects in a mirror have no texture, are merely smooth distortions in the glass. as i should say: *beholder, the magic was inside you all along.* that is, there is no enchantment in the circus. or, there is no circus *but* your enchantment; this frisson is the feeling of one who beholds from a place of relative safety. to run away there must be somewhere to run *from*. this somewhere is also the self.

+

the fairground knows this. the margins know this. the circus knows this. the circus keeps your secrets, beholder, your sugar-rush and sex taboos, arousal and abandonment. the circus is a kind of permission; a kind of itinerant sin-eater. the circus is confined to the outskirts of town. *for a limited time only! roll up, roll up!* and then the circus leaves, and when the circus leaves, it leaves you psychically sated. for the citizen, the circus is an escape from the settled, conventional centre, but the circus is suffered to survive only because it helps this centre to hold. on a certain level the circus is the deepest possible expression of a moral and cultural status-quo.

+

circus? did i say *circus? circus* is a cloudy skin inside of which is starch and fat, mechanically recovered meat; is rusk, husk, and emulsified treyf. the circus is a sausage. by which i mean that *circus* is a word for an illusion; that *circus* will deny its moving parts, that *circus* is a euphemism, a form of abdication, like *porn*, like *capitalism*. i tell her the lion in the circus not an ancient aztec sacrifice, that the lion in the circus is august ames. a sacrifice is special. a circus animal is merely expendable, like all workers, is one among many instrumentalised *others*, is the other whose otherness is an implicit permission to exploit. this applies not only to lions. the circus is a spectacle, beholder, and spectacle at its most fundamental, is a retreat from empathy. of course, this is the crux of our attraction: *cheap holidays in other people's misery.*

+

enchantment is very close to fear, isn't it? what is that pleasurable cold thrill they all talk about? i do not know. as children we are terrified of ghosts. some of us are also mortally afraid of rape. or soldiers. or abduction. or disease. or bombs. sometimes our word for *rape* is *ghost*, sometimes our words *for sickness, indigence, wounding* and *abuse* are *ghost*, and *ghost*, and *ghost*. sometimes it is not *fear of the unknown*. sometimes unknowing is our best defence against fear. a ghost is without motive, pure consequence, cannot and will not be named away. a ghost like dust is residual culture; it carries the accumulative weight of rape and soldiers and abduction and disease and bombs and – sometimes a ghost is evidence, an archive of our own, carried in the occulture of superstition.

+

art is a kind of evidence too, more so music. when it isn't that precipice thrill between self and other, when it isn't beguilingly *wild*, when it isn't trying to seduce you, because you are not its intended auditor. music is the circus talking among itselves. auditor, when i hear the percussive indian drum syllables of hungarian lovara songs, when i hear the slow swooning lilt of *chachi vorba*, when i hear that corruscating balkan brass, played on instruments literally reclaimed from the mud, trampled into the earth by retreating military bands, when i hear *manele* or *chalga* or turbo-folk, when i hear songs in shelta or in irish, when i hear the deliberate seesawing variations of harmony and metre in extemporised sean-nós, i experience this music as an act of both trespass and of exile. these musics are loved into function; their aesthetic shape is forged from centuries of forced migration, dispossession, famine, occupation, and despair. their *mystery* is a rueful ache in me; it is also a hole in the world. adapt to survive, carry what you can, repurpose what you find. a repository for the past, and a fragment of it. *porajmos* means *destruction*, means *cutting up*, means *devouring*. call it *pharrajimos: fragmentation, samudaripen: mass killing.* call it *kali traš: black fear.* songs that bear their otherness before them, an otherness which means that only these songs survive. this otherness has stirred me. i have stood enchanted, but i have stood ashamed and grieving too. for my own lost continuity. for a sensual pleasure born of dread and hunger. for the moments i have made these songs my circus, i am sorry. i should rather heal the hole than have these songs.

+

who are our others if not ourselves? to hear yourself spat back at yourself as a slur or curse. a remnant word for a remnant life. romance too is an operation of power. generations were wearing all their circus on their sleeve. to become a kind of costume. to inhabit the otherness that was forced upon you, until you cannot tell it in the mirror from yourself. until your costume consumes you. until you remove your costume and find yourself not naked but invisible. in the small white boxes at the edge of the fair. step between dogshit and black electrical flex. if some *other* other is moving out there, then it means you no pity, then it isn't a metaphor.

FOR MARTY/ JOURNAL OF LESSER FATIGUES

1:

tricky

the sallow light of my monitor, the recursive anomic monotone of tricky, pursued through looping dehumanised contortions somewhere in the late nineteen-nineties: *can't get no sleep.* the angst-ridden thematics of clubland, fairground, cheap car stereo. atavistic remix, tricky's voice. nocturnal enchantments both carnal and futile. in paranoid ostinato: *can't get no sleep.* nowhere to go, so stagger the marrow-sucked city, shuttered shops, the bleak glyphs of corporate exchange. where sleeplessness concentrates sound, through the grimy polar vortex, via scrub grass, gutless cut-throat buildings. inhale, exhale. an irregular breath, your skin caught in the teeth of a ruined zip. meth. method. through alleyways of mute threat, old meat. canal path, underpass, against the kerb a fox spills out of its own mouth: *can't get no sleep.* the bloody slang of broken teeth. is still twitching, a dull red coat terraformed with mange. eyes like stencils. eyes like stains. reminds me of you. chemical river. twist of glass inside a cloudy marble. drab trysts beneath the bridge. a pirate sky in blue-black brackish waves. junk. the taste of salt and petrol. the marathon: a face up made for grim sybaritic kabuki, a girl drawn on the glass with a stick of rancid mascara. take. double-take. a *shape* but not a *form*, an *i*, not reflected but entrapped. insomnia is *all* surface. smeared across a screen. tricky's voice. the *darkened* affect of a world measured against shame: *can't get no sleep.* our pleasures, clandestine and feral. camden town at three am., the mind, rapt and sullen, the body, arrhythmic, defensive, and slack. a girl on the corner being sullenly pimped. a smell, dogshit on wet crocs. a paper cup held out for change. collects spit, cigarette stubs. we are not nocturnal fetishists. not *drawn* to the night but *driven* to it. rejects. i go round and around. something in the zoo is on fire. the coke-head at the bus stop thinks he's travis bickle, on and on, a long-winded monologue of perpetrator trauma. tricky's voice, slurring like a slow modem: *i can't get no sleep.* in the late nineteen-nineties. sirens. and i want to cry: *cryst hem gyue sorwe*, which is also *fuck the police*, which is also *fuck capitalism*, which is also *fuck the high-alert of lawlessness* on nights i want any oblivion better than this. to consume this circle. zopiclone, risperidone. pac man, eating his way to the centre of a private hell. pac man as outpatient. london. after midnight and forever. i scuttle about in my brain like a spider under a wine glass. pursue the stupid paradox of my own endangerment. because the bed is *not safe*, because the warm room stifles me, because inside there is nowhere to run. the nightworld is flat and vague like a temporary tattoo. empty. dull as a led apron. unless you want what it's selling. and i don't. i don't. return. to the screen. return. tricky recycles exhaustion into fresh resources. writes arousal into anthem, sheds a skin of cold grease, steps unblinking into morning. as hollow as a drilled tooth tricky remakes the world in a warehouse in his wake. *wake* being both aftermath and a sudden coming-to. headphones. *autistic burn-out.* skipping songs. patti smith and a trite little whine about to whom the night belongs. fuck you, patti. the night, heightened and magnified. the body, discordant, unable to integrate. insomnia, in both the production of white suffering and white defiance. condensed against the rhythms of capital. this is old and idiotic. camden town at three am. is not a fucking playground. to occupy the night like you belong is a function of privilege, shit-wits. i fall through these squats, shebeens, kebab shops. the night-bus a lozenge of orange light, moving as slow as a funeral barge. in the shallow light of the monitor, suddenly dead. my own image glitching to me from the late nineteen-nineties: *i can't get no sleep*. insomnia is the present without exit. it is never not happening now. life experienced only through its deferral and affects, as traces.>> you see what i did there?<< my research eats my research. my search, my reach. there is but one moment of eerie bliss: a heron wading in deptford creek. slender witness, minutely adapted to the mercury light of morning. the single thing that belongs in the zombie world between *business* and ~~*pleasure*~~ – *the other thing*. heron does its shimmy, shimmer, little necropastoral boogie. return. again. to the room, to the chair, to the cursor blinking in the stale heat of my prole scrawl always. bulimic spew. i will never be empty enough for sleep. tricky: *i can't get no sleep*. tricky. not a trick, a trap.

2:

god's time

no, *you* shut up. the eunuch faces of policemen, mouths pinched in prim, castrated pique, mouths picked clean of mirth, swaggering at the barricade. or ian paisley jr on the telly, his distended head, the cum face of some agonised ghost. or my students, emailing me at half past eleven at night to tell me they *can't even* over thomas wyatt. gurning through a rictus week again. stale caffeine and curdled adrenalin. i'm all *alone*, i'm *all* alone. prescient pig-fuck, netflix for company. i'll burn my researches, the world is a stage. no, *you* shut up. although yes, the bogey man is capitalism. and being poor you cycle through exhaustion to recovery with no real *leisure* in between. lending and borrowing money has fucked our relationship to time. that is *god's time*. that is season and purpose. now we portion out our days into mingy little units of economic productivity. mercantile time is malignant. debt is a shift in measure and meaning. jesus christ in the temple, losing his shit with a whip of chords because a day should amount to more than an abacus bead, a mark in a ledger, the paranoid accumulation of interest. god *or* money, turd blossom. an imperative between two incommensurable devotions. desire is fucking ontological, okay? or it should be. the orientation of one's being toward whatever. under capitalism, desire is reduced to the *gimme* mottos of spoilt only-children: gratification without satisfaction on an endless frigging loop. and it isn't just that capitalism breaks your knees then sells you crutches – buy noise-cancelling earbuds. buy herbal remedies. buy a lime green sleep-smart memory foam mattress topper, reduced £39.99 – but that it continually recreates the conditions for insomnia, then attempts to put your inability to sleep to work. it's half past two. i'm bug-eyed about borrowing money, marking papers for a school in some other time-zone, replaying the worst moments of my week in a movie montage of grand dysfunction. and no, *you* shut up. because of course i'm angry and this has nothing to do with the fact i haven't slept for more than six hours since last saturday, and anyway it's a mood disorder, not a thought disorder, so you can just – well. at the twenty-four hour tesco fruits and vegetables, sanitised in plastic. the boy stacking shelves has eyes like a myxy rabbit, pink and poorly focussed. there are high ceilings here and a mean, calvinist light over everything. the security guard trails me. anxiety of idleness, awareness of death, and ripples of unrest through every imported item. he glares at me, seems to say mine is a standardised malady, same anarchies of mind as everybody else, a doomed perversity common to all. seems to say: *you're not special*. seems to envy and resent my unproductive shuffle round the rows of chocolate biscuits. fuck him too. you can spend money or you can make money, otherwise *go the fuck to sleep*. i profane the fresh produce with the violence of my thoughts. i don't know why i'm here: *god's time*. i'm not going to complete. it's impossible. my friend says i need to take time off to grieve, and i scream down the phone at her: *what does it look like i'm doing?* she is consumed with the idea of *wellness*, with the kitsch denial of shit that is being *mindful*. with the parcelling out of petty indulgences toward the self. she suggests a sleep app. yes, reconstitute the dormant body as a site of neoliberal control, why not? she says *i don't want to get better*. but better for what? to be a more productive worker, a model citizen, an ideal consumer subject? no thanks. she is scrupulously coddled and i am furious. unseen circuits, hidden networks, irrational, rapidified and geared against our mutual humanity. or, to put it another way: four-thousand packets of identical chocolate biscuits. to put it another way: cocoa slavery. to wake. a surplus of consciousness, of conscience. to tread water and to watch the dead. i tell my friend: *we have to dare to become painfully conscious.* the pope says that when we assume the risk of suffering, when we understand that what is happening to the world is happening to ourselves, when we manifest that, then we will discover what we can do for each other, what we are willing to give. she says: *so? and: fuck the pope. and: what is wrong with you?*

+

okay, let's try this again. suppose insomnia was not the absence of sleep, but it's scar, a remaindered state, a remnant, remnants, fragments, debris. suppose *lack* were the wrong word. think instead in terms of *wound* or *deformity.* a messy psychic excess. a kind of mutilation. what i meant about *laudato si* was this: that capitalism is surrender to rapidity, that oppression is enacted so fast, and our waking hours are so distracted and compressed, that we are never able to entertain another's suffering, to enter their space, to apprehend the slinky little operations of a machine that grinds us all to mince. insomnia makes that space, is a stepping out, is a moral motor too. and she says i'm nuts, and she says i have a bleeding heart as big as a motel waterbed.

+

the brain in its semi-permanent *thester.* theatre and fester, the festering theatre. which is middle english for the obscure side of night. gloomy. gloaming. i sing myself through from crepescule to utmost fuliginy. back when the night had names, had nouns, when you could divide the night into sectional cuts like a dead cow. the modern night is depthless and phobic. no hours of counsel, hours of contemplation, hours of prayer, reprieve. or prey. we are nocturnally illiterate. our best idea is a sex crime behind wheelie bins. we do not know how to love the dark, how the dark might be a journey or a costume. how the night might be consumed, consumes. three hours of sleep. a gold star day in my journal of lesser fatigues. strong coffee, and a student who thinks he's charles bukowski. men. later, a row of aching pussy-hats on the reclaim the night march. middle-class women who think in banner headlines. if it doesn't happen here, it doesn't happen. what would it mean to truly *reclaim* the night? i do not want a sanitary darkness unworthy of the name, but the fulsome return of everything lost. to inhabit the night on its own terms, to unlearn that hateful fear of the dark, which is fear of the other, which is fear as a fetish, which is fear of the self. what does it mean to desire – to truly *desire* – the night for women? a borderless country, a native place. for all us queers. my student, his tedious gap-year amphetamine binge. the language we have for talking about insomnia is woefully imprecise: clinical tongue-clucking that strands us somewhere between a symptom and a cause, or this tom waits bullshit outlaw trope so pungent in cultural memory. the artist: sensitive and extrovert, for whom the usual metabolic laws are suspended, their privilege and stigmata. but insomnia is also the midnight terror of debt; salarymen in blue nylon shirts pulling double-triple-quadruple shifts; the apocryphal coder whose heart exploded into her twelfth red bull. the insomniac is janus-faced, is both decadent and ascetic, both a rebel and a stooge.

+

dymphna, from the irish *damh*, meaning *poet*, is the patron saint of insomniacs, the mentally ill, and victims of sexual abuse. she refused to fuck her father. at the age of fifteen he cut off her head. *and?* she says.

+

no sleep last night or the night before. reading fitzgerald in 'sleep and waking', reading mother theresa on her *long dark night of the soul*. sleeplessness for both of them becomes a *sinister interval*, space of doubt, of numb atheistic preoccupation, all *horror and waste*. fitzgerald drips acid on the psalms: *non timebis a timore nocturno*. for both of them insomnia is kind of proof. that is, an initiation and a grace. *they're not special and neither are you*, she says. in the new house i have an attic office. i tape a quote from djuna barnes to the mirror above my desk: *it is nearer the roof than any other attic in the world. there insomnia is not a malady—it is an ideal.* is that what this is? all of this, my desperate and frustrated attempts to turn malady into ideal? luca on zoom and i say look at that moon, luca, not to be some kind of gooey, moon-maiden cliché about it, but jesus look at that moon. *perversely alert*, it touches that brittle and prolific place in me. it makes a blue flame that wants to write. do the batshit oracular. do rhapsodies. do *some*thing. it saw me standing alone. it demanded action. the moon screamed *jump!*, and i said: how high?

3:
fulsome prison blues

between ardent effort and strictest grief. like a cobalt choke-
hold round my throat. the night. the woman as a line of ants.
the woman as a string of beads. as an urban and mangy
anguish turned inside out. woman as a heap of salt. sleep
is seductive economy. to be blunt beyond language. when
the house has no heat, the mind bisected by cold. on long
nights stiff with necrotic posey, plighting my hygienic troth
to screens. to be a vivid foil among men who know better.
i live through a fresh cut on my thumb and some empathy-
retardant essay on *good (person) poetry*. my sauntering
hormone is my only source of light. what is meant by the
lyric *i* is all the dingy frolics of the self made self, my god,
but the suburbs are leafy tonight. come good in a monologue
of tawdry misdemeanours. and i'm listening to johnny cash,
and fuck you, i'm not a *convict* but a *felon*. when i was a
child i thought the song was *fulsome prison blues*, the surplus
and surpassing blues of carceral time. i thought of the men –
objects without lessons, the stare spilling out of a vacant eye,
of daylight talked into paranoid reversal. i thought of my
father. i talk in wounded tropes. i trump the talking wound.
and a loyalist chant about lead forever. whatever the prison
contains or produces, my song gives up in spades.

+

i shaved my head again. i am told i look like *klaus kinsky's
nosferatu*. i am told i look like *gender-flipped skeletor*. i listen
to the drunks in the park across the street: die kinder der
nacht, welche musik sie machen. or parctice my evil laughter
into the empty office, compose limericks or ditties of minor
humiliation. i invent my own curses by the witch-light of the

monitor –

> my enemy lives
> between the horns
> of a taurian rune,
> affirming thorns.

i am sweaty and crudely seething, *envious*. like all *poor people*. they would only say *i walked in beauty* the way some folk *step in shit*. the world does a denial of violence, does the violence of denial, does the make-work of mockery, day after day. the academics are full of mean, casualised laughter, the cynical reproaches of a worm in warm fruit –

> my enemy's name
> a meet of hounds,
> a face assembled
> round its wounds.

a morning counting cuckoo beads, with fat hands fretting at photocopies. a pink and spatulate melancholy. ugly, like *all poor people*. no one else in the building, just waiting for despair to turn silken. *ríastrad*, a spasm, a true poem –

> my enemy's skin
> is false and pale,
> a shroud cut from
> a canvas sail.

i will raise dogs against swan maidens: white dog of the valley. green dog of the wood. the torn and feathered breath of spring. black dog of death and comic timing. red dog roast on a rowan spit: cú chulainn's doomed taboo. blue-grey dog of dispossession. fine gold dog of flying dust. the final dog they've strained through rubble, even his shadow. *scáth*. runs clear.

+

this meeting could have been an email. then again, your whole life could've been an email. i mean seriously, why bother? sleep and its lack are classed, of course, just as they are gendered and racialised. for us there is no leisure. sleep isn't a sensuous experience in itself. it is only the absence of activity. we've onslaught and exhaustion, oblivion and recovery. when we sleep we are vulnerable. i lie on a squeamish bed and watch the walls heave. i hear every sound outside my window. the poor are positioned as lazy. political discourse frames the lumpen-proles as sleeping, dormant, in need of some external spark. but the poor sleep less than the wealthy. we have been awake too long, we've seen too much. the world happens at me through a sheet of soundproof glass. behind my visor of dull function, i go through the motions. i haven't been paid. i have £0.67. i borrowed money to get into work this morning. and this meeting could have been an email. fuck you, what keeps you up at night?

+

it was after you died, marty, and i'm talking to you now: to keep the night-space sacred to your memory, because the waking world would not permit you, because you'd been gone a month and everywhere they were edging you out. the irrational haunts of the fox are yours, and i love you. the dirtiest talk i know: *i believe in kindness and i'm glad i survived*. it's true, even today. goddess of amnesiac malfunction. bedbug of the deathbed spectacle. spectacle is the opposite of empathy. you, the opposite of empathy. the conscience, doubting crablouse. the conscience, something extinct in a fridge. a shorn moon tonight, and fox on the annex roof in the tenebrous banter darling to vixens. she is more alive than them, crooning their malt distress into lingering iambs. thronged, fatigued, dyspeptic and benighted. where has she been? through the tracksuited slums of boozy return. my fox, somewhere between a *diva* and a *wraith*, more real than them, dragging themselves for years through the dirty reggae of denials, cavils, and cute disclaimers, horny thoughts in a comic font. i thought of you stupidly: *leathchúpla*, a crushed-velvet sibling, my equivalent edge, doubled and repeated. to be libellous, obscene, shrieking out our mutant proofs of joy through days of amputated labour. i thought of you, as i cudgelled the tongue into medicated slang and schlepped myself to counselling. sweating and fretful, trying to be better. when i said myself to typo, rank erratum, humble-brag and shame. a slinky little grimoire bound in my own most orchestrated skin. *poet.* to look on them, to see my own pious manias inverted. silly me, sublimed and vile, scooped off the tarmac. picture this, darling, all of their little-girl soliloquies distilled into a peevish tipple of warm tabasco and bad schnapps, to rivulets of stale mascara, the panda-eyed exaggerations of two am. fox and i are the same, we live in our bodies and not through our scenes. we know the looming future, the looping path, the loping form. circuit without purpose, pursuit without escape. we are not afraid. all they know is the mouth heaped up with smouldering banishments, is anything lullabied, deft against the self and artificing follies in a high lace collar. on a hot, still night in ordinary time, robed in frail affect, robbed of will or reason, a musky stalwart too, skin of ruined sued. how the heart is kitschly pillowed, a feather bed of sullen self-regard. i think about you when i cannot sleep, your gloaming haunches lank with rain. i see the world: legal and stagnant in a spencer tiara, purring its pity-fucks into a flourish. fox and i, a strumpetty moon. bearing the narrow bouquet of ourselves through the past to this place, fractious and rapturing. yes: i believe in beauty, if not for me then for someone else. i don't want to smash what i cannot have. you dug a shallow grave in a hall of mirrors and lay in a bath without water. the sheet works itself into dirty wattles beneath you. you lay on a beach in the raw cold. you never came *home*. i remember a place where men's hands and their lowering humours spilled through the roughness of a council morning, little girls kicked away like crutches, untimely-trimmed, the crust from bread. the longueurs of *deflowering*, summer being tedious and golden, or winter with its griping festive violence and i am anything burnt on a bonfire, the northern air a milky fugue. i cannot sleep, and i am trying to tell you, through the ghetto of my name, through the gulag of your spent and never ending breath. the difference between *useless* and *helpless*. i speak: *labhraím*, through all the melancholy vectors of redress: *labhraím go mall*, inching out over ice into english: *caprice, eclipse, canzone, enclose...* i love what i love, leaking and quickened, and english too for all the fault it finds in me. you looked into you, and found only the licked wound. the fox disappears over the annex roof. tear the paper, stir the coffee, it is okay. how chirst's body befriends my open mouth, and the whole world's a wafer. i've a golden dog and i'm glad i survived, my sideways tidings of comfort and joy.

+

not through its traces
but through its phantoms,
never repeated
but paid back in kind.

horse in its traces,
stamping on atoms.
the greetin and volatile
life of the mind.

for the longest time i made a bolthole of my fury, cut a fairy door in fury so i wouldn't have to feel. i stooped inside of fury and i made myself small. but i know now: crisis and suicidality are perfectly rational responses to a society that doesn't want you to exist. it is sane to desire death in a world that wishes you dead, that tells you this is all you can aspire to. mental health interventions can be life-saving things, but so often treatment centres the root cause of suicidal ideation within the individual. when the root cause is, in fact, the profound injustice of the culture and the political system in which that individual exists. you were *not* ill, you were conscious. you couldn't know what you were conscious *of* because our long, sad history of exploitation and abjection is erased inside this culture, yet you *knew*. your body throbbed with a wrongness we could not name. if i could rewind time, if i could call you back from the brink i'd say just this:

it wasn't you, it isn't us, there was nothing awry with your perceptions, and you were *not* a burden. if it seemed so, if i got frustrated and exhausted with you at times, that is only because friendship and community are the band-aids we use to cover the gaping psychic wounds inflicted by institutional, systemic and cultural abjection. even when i was angry with *you*, i was never really angry with you. i realise now that there is nothing i could have done to fix this, and i realise with equal clarity that there was nothing you could have done to prevent it. that would have required impossible strength of a person already fighting on too many fronts. you had outlived your usefulness to them, they saw no worth in you. the only options for escape or alleviation offered to you served to further the work of annihilation; were both the mechanism of your destruction and their justification for allowing it to happen. i hate this system. it demands impossible things from us because our failure is part of its function. our failure props it all up. and you built their stupid city, you and others like you for generations, with talents and skills they could never hope to possess. you used yourself up building their city, all so they could look down on and discard you. they have their shit meetings in tower blocks they imagine construct and maintain themselves. they tick boxes that destroy you. they live in a fucking dream. they have separated the labourers from the labour and they have excised the poor from poverty. it wasn't you, truly. why are our lives never allowed to be worth anything in and of themselves? i don't know. but if you're told that often enough, what option do you have but to believe it? where are the other stories? where are the generous and spirited reflections of ourselves as vital and alive? were is the future we are allowed to occupy? as ourselves, for ourselves, who cannot and will not become like them? all i want to say is that it's not your fault, and i will never stop raging against this fucking meat grinder as long as i live. when i say FUCK CAPITALISM i am telling you i love you. an all caps love you for the workers, for the poor, for my undocumented tribe. you were *not* instruments or tools. you deserved and deserve so much better than this. than the built-in obsolescence of the body, than their discourses of criminality and contagion, than the bludgeon of othering. when i say i love, you will know what i mean.

ACKNOWLEDGEMENTS

This book owes a debt to Cynthia Cruz' *The Melancholia of Class* (Repeater Books, 2021) for the notion of the working-class 'absent subject' within art and culture.

Some sections of this work first appeared in One Hand Clapping Magazine, the Fortnightly Review and on the Culture Matters website. '"POGGADO JIB"/ DEAR GEORGE' was first published as part of the Darling Delinquents anthology by Sweat Drenched Press.

Excerpts from 'JOURNALS OF LESSER FATIGUES' appear in *Insomnia* (University of Sussex, 2022).

[i] Pierre Bourdieu, *Distinction: a social critique of the judgement of taste* (London: Routledge, 1984) p.190. See also Chris Shilling, *The body and social theory* (London: Sage, 1993).

[ii] Jahan Ramazani, *Poetry of Mourning: The Modern Elegy from Hardy to Heaney* (University of Chicago Press, 1994).

[iii] Charles Eisenstein, *The Ascent of Humanity: Civilisation and the Human Sense of Self* (North Atlantic Books, 2013) p.179.

[iv] Mary Russo, *The Female Grotesque: Risk, Excess and Modernity* (Routledge, 2012) p.8.

[v] Cynthia Cruz, *The Melancholia of Class* (Repeater Books, 2021).

[vi] Gustave Le Bon, *The Crowd: A study of the Popular Mind* (Taylor Francis, 2017).

[vii] Herbert Spencer, *Social Statics Abridged and Revised Together with the Man versus the State*, (BiblioLife, [1892] 2009), p.151

[viii] Douglas Ezzy, 'White Witches and Black Magic: Ethics and Consumerism in Contemporary Witchcraft', *Journal of Contemporary Religion* (2006), 21:1, 15-31, DOI: 10.1080/13537900500381609

[ix] Silvia Federici, *Caliban and the Witch* (Autonomedia, 2004).

[x] Geraldine Monk, *Interregnum* (Creation Books, 1994) p.1

[xi] Joan Dunayer, *Animal Equality: Language and Liberation* (Nature, 2001).

[xii] Dunayer (p.67).

[xiii] Josephine Donovan, *The Aesthetics of Care: On the Literary Treatment of Animals* (London: Bloomsbury, 2016) p.184.

[xiv] Walter Benjamin, *Illuminations: Essays and Reflections* trans. Harry Zohn (Schocken Books, 1969) p.155.

[xv] See Thomas Bartlett, *Ireland: A History* (Cambridge University Press, 2010).

[xvi] Jenny Shaw, *Everyday Life in the Early English Caribbean: Irish, Africans, and the Construction of Difference* (University of Georgia Press, 2013).

xvii See Ken Lee, 'Orientalism and Gypsylorism', *Social Analysis: The International Journal of Social and Cultural Practice* 44, no. 2 (2000): pp.129–56.

xviii See Sarah Sweeney and Billie Dolling for Friends Families and Travellers, 'Last on the list: An overview of unmet need for pitches on Traveller sites in England' (January 202) https://www.gypsy-traveller.org/wp-content/uploads/2021/01/Availability-of-pitches-on-Traveller-sites-in-England_FINAL.pdf

xix Hazel Marsh, 'George Borrow and the Representation of English Gypsies', Journal of the George Borrow Trust (2014).

xx Judith Butler, *Bodies that Matter: On the Discursive Limits of "sex"* (Psychology Press, 1993) p.105.

xxi Martin Hayes, 'where are the working class now', *Underneath* (Smokestack Books, 2021).

xxii *Good White People: The Problem with Middle-Class White Anti-Racism* (State University of New York Press, 2014).